# CONFRONTING DEATH in the School *family*

## Dave Opalewski, M.A.

*and*

## Joel C. Robertson, PHARM.D

**National Center for Youth Issues**

Practical Guidance Resources
Educators Can Trust

ncyi.org

P.O. Box 22185 • Chattanooga, TN 37422-2185
423.899.5714 • 800.477.8277
fax: 423.899.4547 • www.ncyi.org

# Duplication and Copyright

No part of this publication may be reproduced, stored in a retrieval system or transmitted in any from by any means, electronic, mechanical, photocopy , recording or otherwise without prior written permission from the publisher except for all worksheets and activities which may be reproduced for a specific group or class. Reproduction for an entire school or school district is prohibited.

P.O. Box 22185
Chattanooga, TN 37422-2185
423.899.5714 • 800.477.8277
fax: 423.899.4547
www.ncyi.org

ISBN: (10 digit)1-931636-36-2, (13 digit) 978-1-931636-36-0
© 2007 National Center for Youth Issues, Chattanooga, TN
All rights reserved.

Written by: Dave Opalewski, M.A. and Joel C. Robertson, PHARM.D
Cover Design: Phillip Rodgers
Page Layout and Photography by: Jacquelyn Kobet
Published by National Center for Youth Issues

Printed in the United States of America

This manual is dedicated to the compassionate and caring people who work with our greatest national resource—our children.

This manual is dedicated to the compassionate and caring people who work with our greatest national resource—our children.

# Confronting Death In the School Family

## Table of Contents

# Section 3 – Suicide Education and Prevention

© National Center For Youth Issues • www.ncyi.org • 1-800-477-8277
Please refer to page 2 for duplication information

# Section 4 – Suicide Prevention Curriculum

# Section 5 – Crisis Response Planning Worksheets

# Acknowledgments

A manual of this magnitude requires the help and encouragement of many people who work behind the scenes. We feel it important to recognize their contributions in making this project become a reality:

First, we would like to thank our families for their understanding and support during the long hours of research, writing and program development. As we worked with the sensitive and important issues contained within this manual, their enthusiasm for life gave us the motivation to forge ahead with compassion.

We thank Todd Scharich for his countless hours of technical service. His dedication to the objectives of our program was clearly evident through the valuable contributions and sound advice he provided.

Dr. Loren B. Bensley, Jr. was instrumental in encouraging us and providing valued input on various aspects of this program. Being an instructor in Death and Dying, his wisdom is evident in many of the components contained within this manual.

Our many colleagues in the Bridgeport/Spaulding School District, especially Jane Bowns and Bonnie Alexander, deserve recognition for their unwavering encouragement and support.

The Saginaw Intermediate School District provided us with our first opportunity to present this work to school districts located in Saginaw County. Because of their endorsement, many schools that have experienced crises have been able to grow from their experiences.

And finally, to thousands of students, families and patients who have shared their grief and bereavement experiences with us. We learned more from you than we could ever have learned from any other source. Thank you for inspiring us with your courage.

May God bless you all.


Dave Opalewski, M.A.
*Grief Recovery, Inc.*

Joel Robertson, PHARM.D
*Robertson Institute, Ltd.*

# About the Authors

*Dave Opalewski, M.A.*

Mr. Opalewski has been a public school teacher since 1972 and is one of the leading grief recovery experts in the United States. He currently is an instructor for Suicide Prevention and Death Education at Central Michigan University and has taught at the elementary, middle and high school levels. He actively participates in professional forums and is highly sought as a speaker at state and national professional conferences. During his teaching career, Mr. Opalewski has experienced the death of over 25 students and fellow staff members. He also has served as an aftercare consultant for funeral homes, has spearheaded numerous crisis teams for schools and is a widely sought consultant by schools for establishing Crisis Response Programs. Mr. Opalewski is the founder and President of Grief Recovery, Inc., a consulting practice based in Saginaw, Michigan.

*Joel C. Robertson, PHARM.D*

A world-renowned clinician and consultant to the medical, psychiatric and chemical dependency fields, Dr. Robertson has seen more than 11,000 patients, has appeared on television or radio over 1,000 times and is the author of more than 50 books and publications in professional journals. He is President of the Robertson Institute, Ltd., a multifaceted consulting practice based in Michigan, Florida, California and Australia. Dr. Robertson has worked extensively with major corporations and organizations, providing consultation on state-of-the-art physiological and personal enhancement techniques. He is the author of *Peak Performance Living* and *Natural Prozac*.

# Introduction

Imagine this situation. You arrive at school one morning to hear that one of the school's students was killed the night before in a tragic car accident. Then you find out that it was not just any student, but one of your students from your first period class. You remember how smart and outgoing she was. How she was always upbeat and involved, a real prize of a pupil. Why, you just talked with her yesterday afternoon about her class project. And now she's gone!

In a few minutes you will have to face her classmates and deliver the bad news. What will you say to them? How do you explain the unfairness of it all? Should you tell them everything you know about the facts related to the accident? Are there school guidelines you should follow in this situation?

# Purpose of This Program

The death of a student or staff member can devastate a school and its surrounding community. Often these tragedies occur with little or no warning, which means school administrators are left with little or no time to come to terms with the tragedy before they are forced to make decisions that affect the entire community. If you have ever experienced such a crisis, then you know just how painful and difficult it can be.

In recognition of such tragedies and our inability to prevent their happening, we began searching for ways to prepare schools to deal with crises. Our ultimate goal was to provide school personnel with the knowledge, tools and techniques for dealing with any crisis situation. We believe we have met our goal with this program—Preparing for and Responding to the Death of a Student or Staff Member.

This work is based on the belief that the people best equipped to deal with a tragedy in the school are the school's very own teachers, counselors, administrators and staff. You are the school family. As professional as outside counselors may be, strangers cannot exceed the level of trust and respect that you have established with your students and fellow staff members through day-to-day contact. Stated simply, people feel more comfortable talking to friends during a time of crisis.

Therefore, upon completion of this program, your school will have established a tragedy component to your Crisis Response Team that is prepared to handle death and other crises with honesty and compassion. You will plan to help your school remain the physically and emotionally safe environment both students and staff need in a time of crisis. You and your fellow team members will have a better understanding of the grief cycle and the importance of grieving. Finally, should a crisis arise within your school family, your Crisis Response Team will have the knowledge and plans needed to help your students, staff and community to not just survive, but to learn and grow stronger from the experience.

The keys to successfully establishing a sound tragedy component to your Crisis Response Team are organization, preparation and planning. With that in mind, this manual will be your guide. It contains samples of announcements, classroom plans and other materials that can be adapted or duplicated by your team at a time of real crisis. Familiarize yourself with it and refer to it as needed. Your planning will enable your team to respond to any and every crisis in a consistent and compassionate manner.

# How to Use This Manual

This manual deals with four aspects of adding a tragedy component to your Crisis Response Team; Preparation, Implementation, Education, and Prevention. It covers issues you will face including grief lessons for both staff and students, and a curriculum plan dedicated to Suicide Prevention. The authors of this program recommend that each building in the school district have a manual on site, as every school building will need to establish its own Crisis Response Team.

## Section 1: Developing Your Tragedy Component: Planning and Team Preparation

Discusses the need for crisis response planning and the roles of the Crisis Response Team members. It contains the information and gives reference to the forms your team will need to establish a Crisis Response Plan (see Section 5 pages 119-152). Team members should complete all forms referred to in this section.

## Section 2: Implementing Your Tragedy Component: Guidelines and Tools for Specific Situations

Guides your Team through the seven crises that schools most often experience:

1. Student death due to an accident or illness
2. Student death by suicide
3. Student death due to homicide
4. HIV crisis in the school family
5. Staff death due to accident or illness
6. Staff death by suicide
7. Catastrophic death involving several students or staff members

## Section 3: Suicide Education and Prevention

Centers on education and prevention of crisis-related issues including grief management, suicide and memorials.

## Section 4: Suicide Prevention Curriculum

Helps educators and students realize that suicide is an unacceptable, tragic, irreversible act, get assistance for potential suicidal youth, and get in touch with their own feelings on death. It contains lesson ideas for particular subjects that relate to suicide education and prevention.

## Section 5: Crisis Response Planning Worksheets

Contains 20 worksheets originally presented in Sections 2 and 3. These pages may be used as master copies during actual crisis situations.

**NOTE:** The authors and publisher give permission to the owner of this manual to copy the contents of Section 4 as needed for educational and crisis management purposes. These pages are not to be used for resale.

© National Center For Youth Issues • www.ncyi.org • 1-800-477-8277
Please refer to page 2 for duplication information

# IN THE EVENT OF A CRISIS

The most effective way to handle a crisis is to develop a tragedy component to your Crisis Response Team and follow the procedures outlined in Section 2. It is also important to begin incorporating educational efforts on grief and suicide, as described in Section 3.

In the event of a crisis, begin by implementing procedures used in Section 2 for the specific event. This section is intended to be used at the time of the crisis. Within the next week, the prevention and education guidelines located in Section 3 should be, if they have not already been, implemented. Prevention education in Section 3 that already has been implemented should be reviewed. It is essential that procedures in Section 3 be used within the first few days following the original crisis. The educational contents of this section are intended to help reduce the negative consequences associated with a crisis.

# Developing Your Tragedy Component:
## Planning and Team Preparation

The following discusses the need for planning and the roles of the team members. It contains the information and refers to forms your team will need to establish a **tragedy component** to your Crisis Response Plan. **The forms indicated can be found in Section 5 of this book.**

# The Need for Planning

Planning for a future tragedy is neither a pleasant nor desirable chore. It is completely natural to want to avoid such topics as death and suicide, especially when dealing with children. But the facts dictate that this subject merits discussion and action. The reality is that thousands of school-age children die each year. One in every seven children loses someone close to them to death before the child reaches the age of 10.[1] Thousands more experience the expected or unexpected deaths of siblings, grandparents and loved ones. For every one of those children, there are countless friends, classmates and siblings who are left to face their grief and continue living.

Of course schools are more than just students. There are also teachers, support staff, coaches, administrators, counselors and a host of others whose presence and actions support the school family. The loss of any one of these people can devastate a school and the surrounding community.

*We cannot protect our young from the painful realities of life; attempting to do so inhibits growth.* [2]

Now, more than ever, schools function as a second home for children. The classroom offers a structured and supportive environment, the kind that many children are not fortunate enough to experience in their own homes. This is a compliment to the effort that you and our schools put forth to improve the lives of our students.

When a tragedy happens at school or in their home life, children will naturally turn to the most stable force in their lives for support. For instance, if a child loses a grandparent, his or her parents may be incapable of dealing with their own grief, let alone their child's. This can leave children confused, upset and feeling as if they have been abandoned. They will then look to their school family for support.

The same holds true for adults. If you have experienced a crisis or lost a loved one, then you know how important friends and supportive co-workers can be. Birthdays, holidays and special events can be especially difficult when a loved one is no longer alive to share in the celebrations. When situations like this occur, we must remember that grieving is natural and is part of the healing process. The simple acts of listening, understanding and being supportive can have immediate and long-term benefits for both children and adults. These are just a few of the reasons that, as adults entrusted with the health, safety and growth of the next generation, it is our responsibility to prepare for tragic situations.

### A school's goal in dealing with a death should be to:

1. Acknowledge the death honestly.
2. Allow students and staff to express their feelings.
3. Offer an outlet for students and staff who desire to help.

1. National Center for Health Statistics. (1997). Atlanta, GA. Centers for Disease Control and Prevention
2. Wolheit, A. (1996). *Healing and the bereaved child.* Compassion Press.

# Death Experiences

The following experiences are actual cases from one of the authors of this manual. They describe real situations and how they were handled.

**CASE 1**

In October of 1986, the accidental death of a popular eighth grade girl shocked our school. Our principal announced the death over the P.A. system at the beginning of school the following day by saying that "death is a part of life and we have to learn to handle it." Our students were confused and frightened. Social workers were brought in from the outside in case students needed help. No more was said or done by the administration.

**CASE 2**

In February of 1988, a very popular teacher in our district was killed in a car accident. Students and staff were devastated. The building principal called all staff members together to organize a plan. The teacher's personal property was removed from the classroom, and the school physical education teacher (who was well liked by the student body) was temporarily inserted into the deceased teacher's classroom with a sound lesson plan to help the students work through their grief. A staff meeting was called early the next morning to let staff express their grief in the presence of each other and to introduce a plan of action to help the students when they arrived later that morning.

As you can imagine, both of these situations were very difficult to deal with. The first situation demonstrates how a difficult situation can be made even more difficult to bear. The administration's policy to announce the death over the public address system came across as cold and distant. It created a closed feeling for the teachers and staff who felt that the principal had spoken and no more should be said. Teachers were given few official details and were unable to answer the student's questions or calm their fears. Feelings of frustration and anger about the tragedy were heightened by this insensitive approach.

The second situation, although equally as tragic, was handled in a way that was both proactive and sensitive to the needs of staff and students. The principal's decision to call an emergency meeting gave the staff time to deal with the loss, come to terms with the situation and bond to create a plan that would work best for their school. Replacing the deceased teacher with a friendly face made the situation easier on those students. The use of good communication and the administration's acceptance of the tragedy gave the indication that it was okay to grieve.

The sense of togetherness described in the second situation is the one most favored by both faculty and students. In a recent survey of college students who had experienced a death at some point in their scholastic career, 95% of those surveyed did not like the way their school handled the crisis. The reason most cited was their school either did nothing or brought in outside counselors that the students did not know or trust. Respondents overwhelmingly favored the idea of the "School Family Planning" approach.

© National Center For Youth Issues • www.ncyi.org • 1-800-477-8277
Please refer to page 2 for duplication information

# Definition of a "Tragic Situation"

For our intents and purposes, a **tragic situation** can be defined as a *time of great difficulty caused by an unexpected or anticipated death to a member of the school family*. The following is a list of the most common tragic situations. Although the list may be incomplete, the contents of this manual can be adapted or modified by your planning team to any situation.

- Suicide of a student.
- Suicide of a staff member.
- Death of a student.
- Death of a staff member.
- Death of a former student.
- Death of a student's parent, sibling or other family member.
- Ripple effect from a non-directly related tragedy.
- Death of an administrator or significant leader.
- Death of a child or spouse of a staff member.

# The Role of the Crisis Response Team

Upon completion of this program, your Crisis Response Team should be able to provide the following services:

- Serve as a resource to teachers who have questions or who may need help in conducting classroom discussions.
- Assist with small-group counseling.
- Work with students who require additional counseling.
- Work with the classmates of a deceased student.
- Work with classmates of surviving siblings.
- Offer parents an opportunity to discuss ramifications of the loss, characteristics they may wish to watch for in their children and how to further discuss matters with their children. The planning team may assist in the development of materials used to notify parents of this opportunity.
- Identify high-risk students among the close friends of a deceased student.

# Building Your Crisis Response Team

Because a tragedy can happen at any time, it is recommended that a Crisis Response Team be formed in every school building within the district. It is recommended that the principals of each school be co-team leaders with a school counselor, as they are most often seen as the school leaders by students, staff, parents and the community.

The Team Leaders will likely be responsible for selecting the other members for the team, including members to staff the Crisis Rooms. Team members may consist of teachers, counselors, secretaries, coaches, administrators and other willing staff members. It is recommended that copies of the **Tragedy Response Implementation Plan** (page 125) be used in the planning stages here and beyond. Begin by establishing who the Crisis Team members will be. Selection should be based on the following characteristics:

- Team members should be comfortable working together. Because this is often a difficult task that takes place under very difficult conditions, look for team players.
- Team members should be people that the students see every day. Students and staff will need and want to see familiar faces if a tragedy strikes the school family. Simply put, at times of grief we need our friends.
- Team members should be well liked, respected and trusted by students and staff alike.
- Team members should be compassionate. This is a gift that will be vital at a time of crisis.
- Team members should be dedicated. Crises may occur at any hour, so team members must be willing to stay after work or work weekends when needed.
- It is also recommended that the team enlist an outside social worker or psychologist to serve in an advisory position for the Crisis Response Team.

We recommend that members of the Crisis Response Team participate in an in-service training, such as the Grief and Suicide Prevention Training workshops. In-service programs provide a deeper understanding of the grief and trauma associated with loss. This background is helpful for team members when guiding others through crises and making decisions regarding intervention following a death.

# Crisis Response Team Members and Responsibilities

## Team Co-Leaders (Principal, Counselor)

It is the responsibility of the Team Leaders (usually the building principal and counselor) to verify that a death has occurred. When calling parents or relatives of a deceased student or staff member, the team leader needs to state who is calling, indicate the purpose of the call and identify how the information was obtained. The team leaders should inform parents of the steps that the school will be taking and let them know that the school is available to them if needed. It is important that the team leaders be sensitive, reassuring and sympathetic.

The team leaders also need to explain that it would be helpful for the staff and students to receive information about the death and ask the deceased's family for permission to supply teachers with a statement to read in class. Information about funeral arrangements (if known) should be included in the statement. The name of the team's family liaison should be given to the relatives, and they should be told that the liaison will be in contact.

### Additional responsibilities of the Team Leaders include:

- Notifying the superintendent, assistant superintendents and others in the school district.
- Notifying the Media Liaison and Family Liaison.
- Notifying and assembling the Planning Team.
- Scheduling an emergency meeting to inform the staff.
- Hiring substitute teachers to replace Planning Team members.
- Writing an announcement, with input from the Team, to be read in classes.
- Writing and sending a condolence letter to the parents.
- Establishing Crisis Rooms where students and staff can receive assistance.
- Granting staff release time for the funeral.
- Attending the funeral.

A decision to announce the loss at other schools in the district should be made by the Team and the school's administration after assessing the loss and its impact. Telephone contact should be made to other buildings if their staff are to be notified and if their Plans need to be activated.

## Family Liaison

The Family Liaison should be a person who has had contact with the family on previous occasions. Families are usually most receptive to school employees that either they or the deceased had positive experiences with in the past. The impression the family receives from the Family Liaison will be the impression they will have of the entire school's response to the death of their loved one. Therefore, this person must be able to communicate in a sensitive manner. When contacting the family, the Family Liaison should identify himself or herself, express sympathy and share any personal feelings about the deceased.

### Responsibilities of the Family Liaison include:

- Contacting the family.
- Offering to help the family.
  (Suggestions: arranging meals, arranging transportation, running necessary errands, house sitting during funeral, pet care, child-care for siblings, recording of gifts, condolences, and kindnesses extended, etc.)
- Obtaining accurate information from the family.
- Informing the family of school tragedy response plans and procedures.
- Helping the family gather the deceased's personal items from school.
- Attending the funeral.

*continued on next page* ▶

- Keeping in contact with the family after the funeral.
- Following up with key individuals (e.g., friends, parents) of the deceased to make sure they know how and where they may obtain support.
- Providing assistance and referrals for staff members who experience personal trauma related to the loss.
- Requesting further assistance from appropriate outside agencies if necessary.

**NOTE:** If the Family Liaison has not had experience with the person or family in crisis, it would be appropriate to have another staff member who *has* had experience with the family work with the Family Liaison.

# Media Liaison

The Media Liaison should be an individual who understands what information should be given to the media and what is too sensitive for public knowledge. It is strongly recommended that the media not be allowed to roam the school grounds and interview people at will. Mixed messages may occur, and the grieving family may be offended, which would make a difficult situation even worse.

### Responsibilities of the Media Liaison include:

- Making himself or herself known to the media as the school's one and only contact person.
- Supplying media with information pertaining to the crisis.
- Keeping media out of the school.
- Notifying teachers and staff that the Media Liaison is the school's primary media contact.
- Attending the funeral.

**NOTE:** The Media Liaison will need to work in tandem with the Family Liaison to determine what information has been approved by the family to be shared with the media.

# Roamers

Roamers are members of the Crisis Response Team who are present in the halls, interacting with students, during the first few days following a crisis. Roamers should be well known by students and staff and be comfortable communicating with both groups.

### Responsibilities of the Roamers include:

- Being visible in the halls to help maintain order.
- Being in the cafeteria at all student lunch hours.
- Talking with students and staff.
- Escorting students to the Crisis Room if needed.
- Being able to relieve other teachers who may need to go to the Crisis Room or need time alone to express their feelings in private.

- Providing classroom teachers with materials needed for students who wish to create cards for the family.
- Being available to speak to classmates of the deceased's siblings about how to respond upon their return to school. This can be accomplished the first 10 minutes of each class.
- Assisting, in any way possible, in making the grieving process easier.

# Counselors

School counselors are trained listeners and play a vital role in making the Crisis Room a safe atmosphere for students and staff. Counselors can expect students to visit the Crisis Room after the death of a member of the school family. They should encourage students to talk about their feelings and let them know that these feelings are natural. Counselors need to allow students or staff to cry and to show their feelings. They should refer students, if necessary, to available community support resources.

### Responsibilities of the counselors include:

- Staffing the Crisis Rooms.
- Talking with students about the crisis.
- Clarifying misinformation.
- Encouraging students and staff to express their feelings.
- Contacting community support resources, such as specialized counselors and psychologists if needed.
- Providing grief information.
- Making no judgments about individual methods of grieving.
- Providing referrals to community resources.
- Contacting parents if necessary.
- Supporting students.
- Attending the funeral.

# Teachers

Teachers are the primary school contact for the students. Not all teachers will be on the planning team, but all share the responsibility of maintaining a safe and stable environment in the face of a crisis.

### Responsibilities of teachers include:

- Reading announcements and talking with students about the loss.
- Modifying class lesson plans as needed.
- Modifying the time schedule of classes as needed.
- Facilitating activities to encourage expression of feelings.
- Providing grief information.
- Expressing feelings.
- Supporting activities that encourage remembering the deceased.
- Referring students to the Crisis Room if necessary.

*continued on next page* ▶

- Helping create letters of condolence for the family.
- Attending the funeral.

In summary, a **tragedy component** to your school Crisis Response Team provides students and staff with an opportunity to talk through their grief, allowing them to safely express their feelings. Students and staff should have designated Crisis Rooms made available as safe havens for assistance and support. Also, each student and staff member should be given an opportunity to write a condolence letter to the family, participate in remembrance activity planning, and attend the funeral.

# Addressing the Issues

As members of your school's Crisis Response Team, you will not only have to face your own grief, fears and frustrations at a time of crisis, but also act in a way that ensures the safety of your fellow students and staff members. Use this opportunity to think about your roles and responsibilities on the team. Use the **School Faculty and Staff Issues** forms (see page 121) with your fellow team members as you do your planning. This will help familiarize you with the types of questions that will need to be answered in a time of crisis.

**NOTE:** The **School Faculty and Staff Issues** forms (see page 121) will be a vital tool to your team's preparedness in the unfortunate event that you should have a crisis. Familiarize yourself with it now and be prepared to act quickly during a crisis.

# Crisis Room Preparation

Crisis Rooms are assigned rooms, staffed by Crisis Response Team Counselors, where students and staff can go when they need support or privacy while dealing with a crisis. It is the responsibility of those staffing the room to offer help in relation to the crisis, *not* to resolve all of the issues that are happening in an individual's life. If students or staff have additional problems, they should be referred to a community professional.

### Guidelines for staffing the Crisis Room include the following:
- Set up the room for privacy so no one can hear or see those inside.
- Arrange furniture so that conversations can be held without desks or tables between parties.
- Listen to individuals describe their feelings and fears.
- Always have someone available.
- If an individual shares troubling family issues which raise red flags or show signs of suicide, refer the person to a counseling center or private therapist. Document the referral and whether or not the individual accepted it.

© National Center For Youth Issues • www.ncyi.org • 1-800-477-8277
Please refer to page 2 for duplication information

# Counseling a Person In Crisis

The following are suggestions for working with and counseling individuals who are undergoing a crisis situation:

- Encourage them to share personal feelings. Use opening statements such as "How is this situation affecting you?"
- Allow them to remember the person who has died. Do not change the subject. Allow them to discuss the situation, even if it is uncomfortable.
- Do not tell them what they should or should not feel.
- Ask questions about the deceased. Questions such as "Were the two of you close?" show that you care about their relationship and that it was important.
- Share good memories of the deceased.
- Encourage them to engage in a memorial activity.
- Avoid making comments such as "I know how you feel," unless you have truly been in a similar situation.
- If appropriate, share expertise about the grief cycle.
- Say "I do not know," when you cannot answer questions.

If the tragedy was a suicide, probe their own suicide potential by: (1) using the SLAP method described in this manual (see page 149), (2) asking if they would be interested in talking with a professional counselor, (3) making arrangements for students who ask for help and (4) offering a hug if it seems appropriate.

# Community Resources

A list of community resources and individuals is of paramount importance to the Crisis Response Team. Phone numbers of agencies and individuals should be provided to every team member. Agencies and individuals include, but are not limited to:

- County Mental Health Services
- Social Services
- Hospice
- Hospitals (social and spiritual services, psychiatric unit, etc.)
- Psychologists
- Social Workers
- Funeral Directors
- Clergy
- Others

**NOTE:** As you plan with your Crisis Response Team, copy and fill out the **Community Resources Sheet** (see page 119) so that help may be accessed quickly during a crisis.

# Student Funeral Home Visitation

After the tragic death of a classmate or staff member at school, many students may wish (and are encouraged) to go to the funeral home visitation, funeral, or wake service. The crisis team needs to take into consideration that students will need comfort and support at these functions and have an organized system of staff volunteers ready to serve.

> **NOTE:** Some cultures and religions may be very unfamiliar to students. The crisis team should prepare students for the unfamiliar customs and practices of these cultures and/or religions and instruct about appropriate behavior at these functions.

The following is a sample form for a funeral home visitation:

## Funeral Home Visitation Sign-up

Name of Funeral Home: _____

Date: _____     Date: _____

Time: ____:____ AM/PM – ____:____ AM/PM     Time: ____:____ AM/PM – ____:____ AM/PM

| Date | Time | Staff Members | |
|------|------|---------------|---|
| _____ | ____:____ PM/AM to ____:____ PM/AM | _____ | _____ |
| _____ | ____:____ PM/AM to ____:____ PM/AM | _____ | _____ |
| _____ | ____:____ PM/AM to ____:____ PM/AM | _____ | _____ |
| _____ | ____:____ PM/AM to ____:____ PM/AM | _____ | _____ |
| _____ | ____:____ PM/AM to ____:____ PM/AM | _____ | _____ |
| _____ | ____:____ PM/AM to ____:____ PM/AM | _____ | _____ |
| _____ | ____:____ PM/AM to ____:____ PM/AM | _____ | _____ |
| _____ | ____:____ PM/AM to ____:____ PM/AM | _____ | _____ |
| _____ | ____:____ PM/AM to ____:____ PM/AM | _____ | _____ |
| _____ | ____:____ PM/AM to ____:____ PM/AM | _____ | _____ |
| _____ | ____:____ PM/AM to ____:____ PM/AM | _____ | _____ |
| _____ | ____:____ PM/AM to ____:____ PM/AM | _____ | _____ |
| _____ | ____:____ PM/AM to ____:____ PM/AM | _____ | _____ |
| _____ | ____:____ PM/AM to ____:____ PM/AM | _____ | _____ |

© National Center For Youth Issues • www.ncyi.org • 1-800-477-8277
Please refer to page 2 for duplication information

# Crisis Team Plan in Review

The following is a step-by-step format you may follow to develop your school's crisis plan:

- Obtain a charge from your board of education to develop a plan.
- Decide who will be in charge during a crisis.
- Select your Crisis Response Team.
- Develop clear and consistent policies and procedures.
- Provide training for the team and entire staff.
- Establish a working relationship with the police department.
- Select a media liaison and a location to meet the media.
- Make a list of community resources and establish a working relationship with them.
- Create and keep an updated phone tree.
- Develop necessary forms and information sheets.
- Develop a plan for emergency coverage of classes.
- Develop a collection of readings.
- Have all district administrators and board of education review the plan.
- Hold a short annual review meeting.

---

**NOTE:** It is strongly suggested that the school Crisis Response Team meet at least once a year to update the communication phone tree, review policy and procedure, and replace retired staff members serving on the crisis team or members who no longer wish to serve. Not holding this meeting will make it more difficult for the crisis team once a tragedy occurs.

# Implementing Your Tragedy Component:
## Guidelines and Tools for Specific Situations

This section guides your Crisis Response Team through the seven tragedies that schools face most frequently.

# CRISIS 1

# Student Death Due to Accident or Illness

Upon being informed of the death of a student due to accident or illness, the Crisis Response Team should meet and use the **Crisis Response Checklist** (see page 120) as the planning begins. Although this may not be a complete list for all particular situations, the format will help begin the process.

## Staff Meeting

The principal and counselor, as team leaders of the Crisis Response Team, need to call a staff meeting before the students report for school the next day. When scheduling the staff meeting, the leaders need to set aside enough time for the following:

1. Staff to express grief and offer support to one another.
2. Introduction of Crisis Response Team:
   - Explain the roles of team members.
   - Provide a written statement for teachers to read to students. Staff should be free to use other acceptable statements as long as they are sensitive to the situation.
   - Answer questions on procedures.
   - Identify Crisis Room locations.
3. Field questions from staff about how to answer student questions. (The psychologist or social worker serving as an advisor to the Crisis Response Team may lead this discussion.)
4. Make closing comments. Before the staff leaves the meeting, they need to be assured that:
   - Help is available to them as well as the students.
   - They are the key to maintaining a safe environment.
   - The information they have regarding the crisis is accurate.
   - The Roamers in the halls can help get students from classrooms to the Crisis Room and are trained to provide assistance in several ways.

# Statement for Teachers to Read

The following is a sample announcement teachers may read to their classes after a death of a student due to accident or illness:

> **NOTE:** Family Liaison needs to have permission from the family to announce the death at school.

" We are sad to learn that _____(name)_____, in grade_____ , died as a result of (type of accident or illness)   last night. We do not have any more information at this time . . .

(Or)

" We are sad to learn that _____(name)_____ , in grade_____, died as a result of __ (type of accident or illness)_ last night. _(family liaison)_ has talked with the family and this is the information we have at this time .

As more information becomes available, such as funeral arrangements and memorial services, we will pass it on to you. We will be passing out a form called the Student Personal Resource Survey. Please take a few minutes to fill it out. Counselors will be available in a special support room that is for anyone who would like to talk about his or her feelings. Would anyone like to talk about any feelings he or she may be experiencing right now?"

# Sample Letter to Parents

Dear Parents,

We were very sad to hear that one of our students, _____(name)_____, died yesterday as a result of ___(type of accident or illness)___. _____(name)_____ is the son of _____(parents)_____ of _____(address)_____ .

The school's Crisis Response Team has met and discussed a set of planned procedures that have taken or will take place to help our students work through their grief. Counselors and professionals, as well as our trained Crisis Response Team and a caring staff, will be available to students.

**Visitation:**  Smith Funeral Home
Monday, January 5, 1998
2:00 to 5:00 p.m. and 7:00 to 9:00 p.m.

**Funeral Service:**  St. John's Lutheran Church
Tuesday, January 6, 1998
11:00 a.m.

The _____(name)_____ family has invited students to attend the funeral service. Students will be excused from school to do so with parental permission on the signed slip below.

Sincerely,

_____(principal)_____

..........................................................................................................

I, _____, the parent of_____

❑  DO give my permission for my child to attend the funeral service

❑  DO NOT give my permission for my child to attend the funeral service

for _____on _____at_____ .
Signed _____(parent/legal guardian)_____

# Memorials for Death by Accident or Illness

There are many differences associated with handling death from an accident or illness versus death by suicide. The difference between the two should be carefully considered and understood by the Crisis Response Team. The following is a list of actions that a school should consider in the case of death due to an accident or illness. Please note the differences between these procedures and those identified in the section titled "Crisis 2: Student Death By Suicide."

- Provide a moment of silence in the deceased's honor.
- Fly flags at half mast.
- Encourage students or faculty to memorialize the deceased if they so desire. (Their plan should be approved by the Crisis Response Team.)
- Encourage memorials to celebrate the deceased's interests) in life.
- Plant a shrub or tree on school grounds in remembrance of the deceased.
- Memorialize the deceased in the yearbook.
- Enlist groups, such as athletic teams, band or student government, to collect donations for flowers, scholarships or organizations in memory of the deceased.
- Encourage discussion on the cause of death.

# Media Interviews

The following list of suggestions can help the school provide accurate information to the media. This will help minimize the potential for inaccurate reporting, which will avoid further hurt of grieving family and friends.

> Note: The Media Liaison will need to work in tandem with the Family Liaison to determine what information has been approved by the family to be shared with the media.

- Set policies about dealing with the media before a tragedy occurs.
- Direct all media inquiries to the Media Liaison of the Crisis Response Team. This will avoid confusion in times of crisis and guarantee that accurate information is provided to the media.
- Be proactive with the media. Initiate contact with a phone call or press release.
- Use clear, simple language that readers and viewers can easily understand.
- Be polite, professional and courteous to the interviewer.
- Remember that the media has a job to do. View media coverage as an asset to the Crisis Response Team's work.
- Back up facts with original resources. Do not give erroneous information or speculate.
- Make it clear before being taped or recorded that discussion of the details of the cause of the death is not appropriate.
- Avoid sensational or romantic statements.

- Provide only the information that the deceased's family has approved to be made public.
- Do not allow the media to roam the school grounds, interviewing anyone they please. Establish clear ground rules when media are on campus.

## Returning Personal Property

The deceased student may have left items in his or her desk or locker that the family will want to have. The Family Liaison and one of the deceased's favorite teachers should arrange to return the items to the family's home. The items of lesser value may be returned after the funeral, Items of significant value should be returned as soon as possible. Please note: Many students at school know each others' locker combinations. If the deceased does have items of considerable value, the family liaison needs to return them to the family as soon as possible.

Returning items of lesser value after the funeral may be a worthy idea. The visit will likely be appreciated by family members. They may be very emotional and wish to visit for a while as they sort through the items and share their thoughts and feelings. It is important for school representatives to be especially sympathetic and compassionate at this time.

> **NOTE:** Please make use of the **Student Personal Resource Survey** (see page 133) and the **Crisis Response Checklist** (see page 120) as you plan your Crisis Response.

# CRISIS 2

# Student Death Due to Suicide

Upon being informed of the suicide of a student, the Crisis Response Team should meet and use the **Crisis Response Checklist** (see page 120) as the planning begins. Although this may not be a complete list for all particular situations, the format will help begin the process.

## Staff Meeting

The principal and school counselor, as team leaders of the Crisis Response Team, need to call a staff meeting before the students report for school the next day. When scheduling the staff meeting, they need to set aside enough time for the following:

1. Staff to express grief and offer support to one another.
2. Introduction of Crisis Response Team:
   - Explain the roles of Crisis Response Team members.
   - Provide a written statement for teachers to read to students. Staff should be free to use other acceptable statements as long as they are sensitive to the situation.
   - Answer questions on procedures.
   - Identify Crisis Room locations.
3. Field questions from staff about how to answer student questions. (The psychologist or social worker serving as an advisor to the Crisis Response Team may lead this discussion.)
4. Implement the recommended suicide curriculum (see Suicide Prevention Curriculum, page 105).
   - Review **Suicidal Behavior Reporting Form** (see page 135).
   - Review **Suicide Assessment-SLAP Method** (see page 149).
5. Make closing comments. Before staff leave the meeting, they need to be assured that:
   - Help is available to them as well as to the students.
   - They are the key to maintaining a safe environment.
   - The information they have regarding the crisis is accurate.
   - The Roamers in the halls can help get students from classrooms to the Crisis Room and are trained to provide assistance in several ways.

# Student Threatening Suicide

A student threatening suicide, exhibiting self-destructive behaviors or revealing suicidal thoughts through comments, writings, etc., must be taken seriously. It is to be assumed that this student could act out the threat. The following are guidelines for dealing with a student threatening suicide.

- Immediately notify the school principal, using the "**Suicidal Behavior Reporting Form**" (see page 135).
- The principal should choose a person or persons to stay with the student during the crisis period, and contact the student's parents. The principal should provide the parents with a description of the incident and an explanation of the school's concern. Certain qualified staff members should also be made available to communicate with the family.
- The parent(s) should be advised to pick up their child at school. The student should not be left alone until the parent(s) arrives. The parent(s) should complete the "**Parental Agreement/Release Form**" (see page 137) when picking up the child.
- If a parent cannot be reached, the principal should call community resources (e.g., county mental health, hospital psychiatric unit, or student's church minister).
- The Crisis Response Team should be called on to provide assistance to staff, students and the suicidal student's family.
- The Crisis Response Team should follow up the incident with a report to the superintendent, using the "**Suicidal Behavior Reporting Form**" (see page 135), and place a copy of the report in a confidential file.

# Attempted Suicide On School Property

If a person self-inflicts an injury, and the injury is perceived as life threatening (e.g., bleeding, drug overdose), call 911 or Emergency Medical Services immediately. The building principal should be notified and the following procedures implemented:

1. Provide the name and age of the student and nature of the concern (i.e., injury or substance abuse). If substance abuse, the principal needs to inform the 911 operator of the student's state of consciousness and save any evidence of the suspected substance ingested for the Emergency Medical Services.
2. Remove other students and assign a staff person to stay with the student until arrival of the Emergency Medical Services.
3. Contact the student's parents and direct them to the medical facility to which the Emergency Medical Service unit is taking the student.
4. Write a follow-up report to the superintendent, using the "**Suicidal Behavior Reporting Form**" (see page 135), and place a copy of the report in a confidential file.

The Family Liaison should contact the family to offer assistance. Students who have attempted suicide on school property should not be allowed to return to school until written permission is provided to the building principal by a certified counselor, psychologist, social worker or psychiatrist, stating specifically that the student is prepared to return.

# Statement for Teachers to Read

The following is a sample announcement teachers may read to their classes after a death of a student due to suicide:

> **NOTE**: The Family Liaison needs permission from the family to announce the death at school.

"As you all know by now, _____(name)_____ took his(her) life last evening. _____(name)_____ was a person who was really hurting inside. The action he(she) took was the result of this pain. This action is inappropriate. Let us not judge _____(name)_____ to be a bad person, but realize that there are more positive ways to handle our problems. We have all lost a friend and are hurting. When people take their lives, they hurt their families and friends too. Although we are sure _____(name)_____ never meant to hurt anyone, his(her) family and friends are now hurting. Let us all understand that there are a lot people who care about us and are willing to listen and help.

In handling your grief, I want you to understand the following points:

- We all have problems.
- Our problems do not last forever. Dark days will pass.
- Suicide is never an answer to our problems.

We will be handing out a form called the Personal Resource Survey. Please take a few moments to fill it out. Counselors will be available in a special support room for anyone who would like to talk about his or her feelings. Thank you."

**(or)**

"Yesterday afternoon, at approximately _____(time)_____, a tragedy occurred involving _____(name)_____. We all know that no one single incident or situation causes a person to commit suicide. We will never know all the reasons for _(name)_ actions. It is important to realize that we must reach out to each other at this time, be friends, listen, care and help each other understand and realize that each one of us is important. In the days ahead, take time to tell one another that you care. We will be handing out a form titled the Personal Resource Survey. Please take a few moments to fill it out. Counselors will be available in a special support room that is for anyone who would like to talk about his or her feelings. Thank you."

After reading one of the above statements, allow students to discuss the tragedy if they wish. As they talk, keep the following in mind:

- Encourage students to express their feelings.
- Try not to let the discussion glamorize the act.
- Remind students that no one person is responsible.
- Reinforce that suicide is a tragedy. Do not allow someone to become larger in death than they were in life.
- Suicide does not solve problems. It creates them. Suicide is a permanent solution to a temporary problem.

*Take special note of students who appear unusually upset by this discussion. Make referrals if necessary.*

# Sample Letter to Parents

The following is a sample letter the school can mail to parents after a suicide. It is strongly suggested that before this letter is mailed, *all facts are verified and permission to announce the suicide has been granted by the family of the student.*

Dear Parents,

We are very sad to announce that ___(name)___ took his(her) life on ___(date)___. Suicide is always a very tragic and traumatic event in the school community. We are aware that grief due to suicide is different from grief due to death from natural causes.

Our Crisis Response Plan has been activated to maintain a safe and calm environment at school. Our emphasis at school will be to assist our students and staff in expressing their grief appropriately and to educate them in the area of suicide prevention. The staff have classroom discussion activities designed to accomplish these goals. Our counseling staff and the Crisis Response Team will also be available for assistance. We will do our best to help our students express their emotions and encourage them to be kind to themselves. We are on the alert for possible copycat behaviors and will arrange for these individuals to receive assistance.

As a parent, we encourage you to talk with your children about this tragedy. Allow them to express their feelings and concerns. Reaffirm your love for them and reassure them that you are willing to listen to their fears and problems.

Please feel free to call me if we can be of more assistance.


Sincerely,


(Principal)

## Guidelines for Schools After Suicide

When a student commits suicide, there is sometimes a fear that other students will follow the example and also attempt suicide. Given that such copycat suicides have occurred at several schools across the country, these concerns are justified. Schools should be concerned about their role in preventing such copycat behavior. The following is a list of suggestions for school personnel to consider:

- Consider how to respond to the death of a student or staff member before a suicide occurs. The Crisis Response Team should develop plans for different situations.

- If a suicide does occur, activate the Crisis Response Team's plan immediately.

- Give friends who were closest to the deceased additional time and help to process the suicide. Try to bring as many of them together to share what they know of the deceased and to help explain why he/she would do such a thing. This may help relieve guilt and build a sense of support for one another. Stress that the deceased would have been better off if he/she had talked about his/her problems. Encourage them not to make the same mistake.

- Plan a presentation about general suicide information for teachers and students.

- Provide an opportunity in the classroom for students and teachers to discuss their feelings about suicide. Make sure that everyone knows that what they are feeling is normal. It is important to create an environment that is open to, but not critical of, the feelings of others.

- Remember that it is not only the friends of the deceased who may be at high risk for copycat behavior. For students who have been troubled and depressed, suicide sometimes can reinforce feelings that the world consists only of problems and pain.

- Schedule a meeting with parents to discuss the suicide. They will likely want to ask questions, talk about their feelings and be advised about what to say to and watch for in their children. Inform parents about community resources that are available to them and their children.

- Inform teachers to watch students' stories, reports and drawings for clues of depression and suicidal thoughts.

- Provide opportunities in course offerings (e.g., Health Education, Social Studies, Home Economics) to teach positive problem-solving skills.

- Inform students that while guilt can be a natural feeling following a suicide, the suicide was the choice of the person who committed the act. No one else is responsible.

## Classroom Suicide Discussion

In the event of a student suicide, shock will certainly be apparent. Students and staff may be unable to say anything about the event at all. They may show no outward emotion or appear overwhelmed with sorrow. The following guidelines will assist students and staff in being able to talk about the tragic event:

- Have teachers calmly read the announcement provided by the Crisis Response Team at the set time.

- Allow a minute for the news to sink in, then ask if anyone has any statements or questions. If questions cannot be answered, they will need to be written down and answered later.

- Let the students know that the next few days and weeks will be a period of adjustment for everyone, including the teachers. Make it known that everyone will need each other's support and that they should not hesitate to ask for some time to talk about their feelings.

- Stress that many feelings will probably surface in the next few days including fear, anger and a sense of loss. Acknowledge these feelings (especially anger) as a normal part of the grieving process.

- Stress that it is common for people to think about suicide on occasion. Stress that if any one is preoccupied with suicidal thoughts, he or she needs to talk to the individuals in the Crisis Rooms. Make sure that Roamers are available to escort students to the Crisis Room.

- Explain to students that if they know someone who is thinking about suicide, they must not keep it secret. If they keep it a secret, a friend could be lost forever.

- Allow students to comment on what they are feeling. Allow time for any discussion that students may need.

- Move back to regular class work when it is appropriate to do so. A balance must be struck between the students' need to talk and the need to show that the world will continue. It is important not to glorify suicide, which can make it more attractive than life for some troubled people.

- Watch for students who have an unusual reaction to the news of the event (i.e., students who show either no emotion, or overwhelming sadness). Report these students to the counseling staff.

- Show concern, ask questions in a straight-forward manner and be willing to discuss the tragedy. Evaluate students' reactions in order to get them help if they need it.

## Classroom Suicide Discussion Questions

A suicide crisis in the school setting should be talked about, with every individual being free to speak or just listen. Teachers may need to share their feelings first to get students involved. These questions are meant to help students develop a better awareness and understanding following a suicide.

- What thoughts and feelings might be involved in someone wanting to commit suicide?
- What might cause a person to have such thoughts and feelings?
- What must it be like for someone to have these thoughts and feelings?
- What were some of your thoughts and feelings when you first heard the news?
- What possible purpose might a person have for committing suicide?
- What might a friend or classmate do for a friend who is suicidal?
- Do you find yourself thinking and feeling differently about suicide now than when we first started talking about this?

Summarize the key points made and leave the door open for discussion.

# Grief Reactions of Survivors of Suicide

When helping friends and classmates of a suicide victim, it is important to know what reactions to expect. The following reactions are normal ways of coping and part of the overall healing process:

- *Shock* – A sense of numbness or lack of feeling. The belief that what has happened is not real.
- *Denial* – Having a difficult time believing that a person is really dead even though they are aware of the reality.
- *Guilt* – Usually one of the first feelings to be experienced after suicide and one of the last with which to be dealt. The survivors' guilt is relieved when they come to the realization that the suicide was the choice of the person who committed the act. We are not responsible for other people's actions.
- *Emotional outburst and irritability* – Survivors may experience outbursts of crying, anger, denial, guilt, shame, panic and fear. Because of stress, people may become more impatient, irritable and restless. All these may lead to disrupted sleep and eating patterns.
- *Depression or sadness* – After weeks of the above feelings, survivors may become emotionally drained and depressed. This can last for weeks or months, with good days occasionally happening.
- *Anger* - Anger towards the deceased is common. Often this emotion is the result of people's grieving for themselves, rather than for the deceased.

# Help for Survivors of Suicide

The following guidelines can be helpful for students and staff who want to help others struggling with a friend's suicide:

- Initiate conversation about the suicide and let them know that their grief is different than if the death occurred through natural causes. Do not be afraid to use the word suicide. This helps to desensitize individuals and allow them to face the reality of what happened.
- Do not assume you know how they feel. Just listen patiently, without being judgmental.
- If someone feels guilty, let them know that the death was not their fault. The individual made the choice to commit suicide.
- Provide them with information about suicide and grief. The school's Crisis Response Team should have information available.
- Do not let them feel that they are alone. Help them realize that others have gone through similar experiences and survived.
- Give them permission to be angry at the deceased, to cry and to experience all other emotions they may have.
- Let them know that this will be a very stressful time. Encourage them to be kind to themselves and to eat and sleep well.
- Do not try to answer the question if they ask "Why?" Survivors will ask this question over and over and may answer part of the question on their own. The question, however, can never be fully answered.

- Recognize that survivors are often angry at what happened and may take their anger out on staff. Try to be patient and understanding.
- Sometimes the survivors become suicidal themselves. Watch for clues and do not be afraid to ask them how they feel and if they have thoughts of dying.
- Inform them that the grief process is a long one. Many have found that they are able to reconnect back into daily living after an average of 24 months. It should be noted, however, that the pain of the loss will probably be with them throughout their lives.

## Memorial for Death Due to Suicide

There are many differences associated with handling a death from suicide versus death from other causes. These differences should be carefully considered and understood by the Crisis Response Team. The following is a list of actions that your Crisis Response Team should consider.

> **NOTE:** these suggestions differ greatly compared to the memorial procedures identified in the **"Crisis 1: Student Death Due To Accident Or Illness."** This is to avoid glamorizing suicide in any and every way.

- Do not announce the death over the P. A. System or conduct a moment of silence.
- Do not lower flags to half mast.
- Avoid school sanctioned tributes, memorials or events.
- Close friends who wish to remember the deceased in a special way should be encouraged to do so in a quiet way that celebrates life (e.g., purchase of a video on suicide prevention, a researched publication of a list of teen resources, etc.).

In the handling of death by suicide, the Crisis Response Team may need to explain these procedures. The reason: To discourage memorializing, to avoid glamorizing, romanticizing or in any way encouraging suicidal behavior.

## Media Interviews

The following list of suggestions can help the school provide accurate information to the media. This will help minimize the potential for inaccurate reporting, which will help avoid furthering the hurt felt by the grieving family and friends:

> **NOTE:** The Media Liaison will need to work in tandem with the Family Liaison to determine what information has been approved by the family to be shared with the media.

- Set policies about dealing with the media before a tragedy occurs.
- Direct all media inquiries to the Media Liaison of the Crisis Response Team. This will avoid confusion in times of crisis and guarantee that accurate information is provided to the media.
- Be proactive with the media. Initiate contact with a phone call or press release.
- Use clear, simple language that readers and viewers can easily understand.
- Be polite, professional and courteous to the interviewer.

*continued on next page* ▶

- Remember that the media has a job to do. View media coverage as an asset to the Crisis Response Team's work.
- Back up facts with original resources. Do not give erroneous information or speculate.
- Make it clear before being taped or recorded that discussion of the details of the cause of the death is not appropriate.
- Avoid sensational or romantic statements.
- Only provide information that the deceased's family has approved to be made public.
- Do not allow the media to roam the school grounds, interviewing anyone they please. Establish clear ground rules when media are on campus.

**NOTE:** Discuss with the staff the need to review the school's policies on weapons, violence and overall school security. Consider forming a Conflict Resolution Team.

## Dealing With the Siblings of the Deceased

- Debrief the student before they come back to school following the incident.
- Have a plan in place to offer support to the student in the event that he or she becomes overwhelmed by grief during the school day. Discussing this support plan with the student **before** there is an upset will help them feel more comfortable and secure.
- Don't draw attention to the student if he becomes over-whelmed by his grief.
- Guide fellow classmates on how to be supportive and understanding before the student returns to school.
- Keep communication open with the family and discuss any issues you might see in the student.

## Returning Personal Property

The deceased student may have left items in his or her desk or locker that the family will want to have. The Family Liaison and one of the deceased's favorite teachers should arrange to return the items to the family's home. These items should be returned after the funeral, unless they are of significant value.

The visit will likely be appreciated by family members. They may be very emotional and wish to visit for a while as they sort through the items and share their thoughts and feelings. It is important for school representatives to be especially sympathetic and compassionate at this time.

Note: Make use of the **Crisis Response Checklist** (see page 120), the **Student Personal Resource Survey** (see page 133), the **Suicidal Behavior Reporting Form** (see page 135), and the **Parental Agreement/Release Form** (see page 137) as you plan for this crisis.

# Student Death Due to Homicide

There are two types of situations that involve the death of a student by homicide: (1) those that occur outside of the school property, and (2) those that occur on the school grounds. Hysteria and fear will exist in both situations. A homicide on the school grounds, however, generally results in greater hysteria, fear and insecurity for a longer period of time.

If the homicide occurs on school property, the school will need to address the future safety of its students. Policies and procedures for handling violence may need to be reviewed and additional safeguards provided to the students, staff and community. In this section, procedures to address the community are presented. In all cases of on-school-property homicides, the community should be involved. In some cases of off-school-property homicides, the concerns of the community pertaining to the welfare of the children will need to be addressed.

The Crisis Response Team will need to meet and discuss the situation and develop recommendations for the school's administration. If violent confrontations occur with any frequency in the school, the Crisis Response Team should strongly suggest that a Conflict Resolution Team be formed in the school. (Conflict Resolution Teams will be discussed later in this section.)

Upon being informed of the homicide of a student, the Crisis Response Team should meet and use the **Crisis Response Checklist** (see page 120) as the planning begins. Although this may not be a complete list for all particular situations, the format will help begin the process.

# Staff Meeting

The principal and school counselor, as team leaders of the Crisis Response Team, need to call a staff meeting before the students report for school the next day. When scheduling the staff meeting, they need to set aside enough time for the following:

1. Allow staff to express grief and offer support to one another.

2. Introduction of the Crisis Response Team:

   - Explain the roles of Crisis Response Team members.
   - Provide a written statement for teachers to read to students. Staff should be free to use other acceptable statements as long as they are sensitive to the situation.
   - Answer questions on procedures.
   - Identify Crisis Room locations.

3. Field questions from staff about how to answer student questions. (The psychologist or social worker serving as an advisor to the Crisis Response Team may lead this discussion.)

4. Closing comments. Before staff leave the meeting, they need to be assured that:

   - Help is available to them as well as the students.
   - They are the key to maintaining a safe environment.
   - The information they have regarding the crisis is accurate.
   - The Roamers in the halls can help get students from classrooms to the Crisis Room and are trained to provide assistance in several ways.

© National Center For Youth Issues • www.ncyi.org • 1-800-477-8277
Please refer to page 2 for duplication information

# Statement for Teachers to Read

The following is a sample announcement teachers may read to their classes after a death of a student.

> **NOTE:** Family Liaison needs to have permission from the family to announce the death at school.

"We are sad to learn that _____(name)_____, in grade_____, was killed last night.

We do not have any more information at this time . . .

*(Or)*

We are sad to learn that_____(name)_____, in grade_____, was killed last night.

_____(family liaison)_____ has talked with the family and this is the information we have at this time.

As more information becomes available, such as funeral arrangements and memorial services, we will pass it on to you. We will be passing out a form called the **Student Personal Resource Survey** (see page 133). Please take a few minutes to fill it out. Counselors will be available in a special support room that is for anyone who would like to talk about his or her feelings. Would anyone like to talk about any feelings he or she may be experiencing right now?"

**CRISIS 3**

## Sample Letter to Parents

The following is a sample letter the school can mail to students' parents after a homicide. It is strongly suggested that before this letter is mailed, *all facts are verified and permission to announce the student's death has been granted by the family of the student.*

Dear Parents,

We were very sad to hear that one of our students, _____(name)_____, died yesterday as a result of homicide. _____(name)_____ is the son of ___(parents)___ of _____ (address)_____.

The school's Crisis Response Team has met and discussed a set of planned procedures that have taken or will take place to help our students work through their grief. Counselors and professionals, as well as our trained Crisis Response Team and a caring staff, will be available to students.

**Visitation:**    Smith Funeral Home
         Monday, January 5, 1998
         2:00 to 5:00 p.m. and 7:00 to 9:00 p.m.

**Funeral Service:**  St. John's Lutheran Church
         Tuesday, January 6, 1998
         11:00 a.m.

The _____(name)_____ family has invited students to attend the funeral service. Students will be excused from school to do so with parental permission on the signed slip below.

Sincerely,

___(Principal)___

· · · · · · · · · · · · · · · · · · · · · · · · · · · · · · · · · · · · · · · · · · · · · · · · · · · · · · · · · · · · · · · · ·

I, _____, the parent of_____

❏  DO give my permission for my child to attend the funeral service

❏  DO NOT give my permission for my child to attend the funeral service

for _____on _____at_____.
Signed _____(parent/legal guardian)_____

© National Center For Youth Issues • www.ncyi.org • 1-800-477-8277
Please refer to page 2 for duplication information

# Student Violence Advisory Committee

If your district does not have a Student Violence Advisory Committee, the Crisis Response Team should recommend that one be formed. Typically, these committees are commissioned by the board of education. They should include law enforcement professionals, members of the Crisis Response Team, parents, teachers, attorneys and students. The purpose of this committee is to:

1. Recommend that specific policies to deter violence be considered for adoption by the school board. These policies could be included in the parent/student handbook.
2. Develop an in-service training for all school personnel (including members of the board of education) concerning issues of safety, prevention of violence, death and bereavement. This training should be specifically geared toward establishing and maintaining a safe environment and allaying fears of the students, staff and community.

# Special Action Plans Following a Homicide

The following suggested activities are aimed at helping school administrators handle the major concerns of students, staff and the community. It is suggested that these action plans be implemented if the homicide occurs on school property. In situations where fear and hysteria are high within the community, the following plans would also be appropriate.

### Staff and Student Body

*Emergency Staff Meeting* – Before students arrive for school.

1. Explain the plan of action to staff.
2. Answer any pertinent questions.
3. Adjust time schedules due to student assembly.
4. Review the worksheet and directions for teachers to use in homeroom following the assembly.
5. Outline procedures for dismissing classes from homeroom for an abbreviated school day.

*Student Assembly* – Attended by the whole student body, if possible.

1. Clarify the situation.
2. Include presentations by law enforcement professionals on how to maintain a safe environment and lifestyle.
3. Begin discussion, led by school official or principal, on policies to ensure the safety of the school family.
4. Answer any pertinent questions from the student body that will not be covered in homeroom.
5. Announce rules and procedures that will be, or have been, implemented that are geared to ensuring safety. Such rules and procedures might include the following:
   • Zero tolerance for fighting.
   • A ban on gang signs, colors, jackets, etc.
   • School-wide dress code or uniforms.
   • Drive-by shooting drills (similar to tornado and fire drills).

- Metal detectors or book bag inspections.
- Establishment of a Conflict Resolution Team.

6. Dismiss students to homeroom for related activity (see **Student/Teacher Worksheet for Homicide Assembly**, page 139).

## Community Activity

The day of or following a homicide, the Crisis Response Team and Student Violence Advisory Committee (if available) should be present for a community meeting in the evening. The agenda for the meeting should allow time to do the following:

1. Clarify the situation.
2. Explain the school administration's major goals:
   - Develop prevention policies to help students develop a safe attitude and ways to live a safe life.
   - Prevent and eliminate fear and hysteria.
   - Maintain a safe and stable school environment for all.
3. Announce possible new rules and procedures to create a safe and stable school environment.
4. Answer questions from the audience.

# Conflict Resolution Teams

Conflict Resolution Teams are used to prevent violence on school property and help develop rules and procedures that can improve the safety of the school. The team should consist of at least two members and be involved in resolving any conflicts that may arise. It is recommended that the Conflict Resolution Team establish a working relationship with local law enforcement. Law enforcement officers may even volunteer to serve on the team in advisory roles.

From monitoring the halls between classes to helping patrol parking lots, Conflict Resolution Teams can improve the safety of schools in many ways. One of the most important may be in the area of educating students to resolve conflicts in an appropriate way. This may be done in small groups, such as in homerooms, Social Studies or Health Education classes. Conflict resolution programs should incorporate the following:

- Explaining to students that it is okay to disagree, but violence is never acceptable.
- Teaching young people how to disagree.
- Educating people about the short-term and long-term effects of violent behavior.
- A student mediation program.

## Student Mediation Program

In the student mediation program, disputing students meet with an unbiased mediator. Students who participate as mediators will need to be mature enough to keep all conversations confidential, and listen to both sides of the story without interrupting. The student mediator will then help the two opposing students brainstorm possible solutions. The students create a solution to which they both can agree and sign an agreement stating the specifics.

© National Center For Youth Issues • www.ncyi.org • 1-800-477-8277
Please refer to page 2 for duplication information

This type of program has shown to be very effective in schools where the students are challenged to make it work. Before allowing students to mediate, however, they should be trained by qualified personnel and function under the supervision of a trained staff member.

## Memorial for Death Due to Homicide

The death of a student is always painful. When that death is due to homicide, feelings of hurt are often accompanied by fear. More so, when law enforcement comes up with few clues and fails to make an arrest in the case. In any event, a memorial service is recommended to help surviving friends and classmates come to terms with the loss. Memorials also give people something positive by which to remember the deceased. Because memorial services often bring out deep emotions in people, it is recommended that members of the Crisis Response Team and counselors be present and available to help those who need it. The following is a list of actions for schools to consider in the event of a death due to homicide.

- Provide a moment of silence in the deceased's honor.
- Fly flags at half-mast.
- Encourage students or faculty to memorialize the deceased if they so desire. (Their plan should be approved by the Crisis Response Team.)
- Encourage memorials to celebrate the deceased's interest(s) in life.
- Plant a shrub or tree on school grounds in remembrance of the deceased.
- Memorialize the student in the yearbook.
- Enlist groups, such as athletic teams, band or student government to collect donations for flowers, scholarships, or an organization in memory of the deceased.
- Encourage discussion on the cause of death.

## Media Interviews

The following list of suggestions can help the school provide accurate information to the media. This will help minimize the potential for inaccurate reporting, and avoid furthering the hurt felt by grieving family and friends.

Note: The Media Liaison will need to work in tandem with the Family Liaison to determine what information has been approved by the family to be shared with the media.

- Set policies about dealing with the media before a tragedy occurs.
- Direct all media inquiries to the Media Liaison of the Crisis Response Team. This will avoid confusion in times of crisis and guarantee that accurate information is provided to the media.
- Be proactive with the media. Initiate contact with a phone call or press release.
- Use clear, simple language that readers and viewers can easily understand.
- Be polite, professional and courteous to the interviewer.
- Remember that the media has a job to do. View the media coverage as an asset to the Crisis Response Team's work.

*continued on next page* ▶

- Back up facts with original resources. Do not give erroneous information or speculate.
- Make it clear before being taped or recorded that discussion of the details of the cause of the death is not appropriate.
- Avoid sensational or romantic statements.
- Only provide information that the deceased's family has approved to be made public.
- Do not allow the media to roam the school grounds, interviewing anyone they please. Establish clear ground rules when media are on campus.

## Dealing With the Siblings of the Deceased

- Debrief the student before they come back to school following the incident.
- Have a plan in place to offer support to the student in the event that he or she becomes overwhelmed by grief during the school day. Discussing this support plan with the student **before** there is an upset will help them feel more comfortable and secure.
- Don't draw attention to the student if he becomes overwhelmed by his grief.
- Guide fellow classmates on how to be supportive and understanding before the student returns to school.
- Keep communication open with the family and discuss any issues you might see in the student.

## Returning Personal Property

The deceased student may have left items in his or her desk or locker that the family will want to have. The Family Liaison and one of the deceased's favorite teachers should arrange to return the items to the family's home. These items should be returned after the funeral, unless they are of significant value.

The visit will likely be appreciated by family members. They may be very emotional and wish to visit while they sort through the items and share their thoughts and feelings. It is important for school representatives to be especially sympathetic and compassionate at this time.

> **NOTE:** Make use of the **Crisis Response Checklist** (see page 120), the **Student Personal Resource Survey** (see page 133), and the **Student/Teacher Worksheet for Homicide Assembly** (see page 139) as you plan for this crisis.

© National Center For Youth Issues • www.ncyi.org • 1-800-477-8277
Please refer to page 2 for duplication information

# CRISIS 4

# HIV Crisis In the School Family

The following strategies and recommendations for dealing with an HIV-positive student in the school family are only to be used if the infected student and his or her family are willing to make the information public (or have already done so). This section is not intended to be a curriculum or educational program on HIV/AIDS, but rather presents procedures that will encourage positive attitudes toward the HIV-positive student. When implemented, this program should help prevent infected students and their families from enduring the ridicule and humiliation that other students, such as Ryan White, have experienced. It should also help school personnel prevent and reduce hysteria surrounding HIV/AIDS and maintain a safe and stable environment.

An HIV/AIDS Advisory Committee should be established for the school district and commissioned by the board of education. It is suggested that this committee be made up of health care professionals, parents, Crisis Response Team members, teachers, attorneys and students. The purpose of this committee is to:

1. Recommend policy statements about HIV/AIDS to be considered for adoption by the school board. A public meeting might be considered to gain community input. These policies could be included in each school's parent/student handbook.

2. Research and oversee an in-service training program for all school personnel, including the board of education, concerning HIV/AIDS issues, including transmission, prevention, civil rights, mental health, death and bereavement. This training should be specifically geared toward staff member's knowledge, feelings, attitudes, behavior and acceptance of people who are infected with HIV.

3. Recommend precautions relating to blood-borne infections. OSHA already has established guidelines for health care facilities that could be easily adapted for use by schools. Regardless, there should exist a system for quality assurance or monitoring to document compliance with all precautions adapted by the district.

## Administration Concerns

1. Safety of all students, *including* the HIV-positive student.
2. Student body reaction.
3. Community reaction.

## Action Plans

The following suggested activities are aimed at helping the school administration handle the three main administration concerns. These activities may be altered to fit individual situations.

### Staff and Student Body

***Day One***: **Emergency Staff Meeting** – Before students arrive for school.

1. Explain the plan of action to staff.
2. Answer any pertinent questions.
3. Adjust time schedules due to student assembly.
4. Review the worksheet and directions for teachers to use in homeroom following the assembly.
5. Outline procedures for dismissing classes from homeroom for abbreviated school day.
6. Hold a short faculty meeting following the end of the school day to discuss any student or staff concerns and the schedule for the next day.

***Day One***: **Student Assembly** – Attended by the whole student body, if possible.

1. Clarify the situation.
2. Have a presentation by a health care professional about how HIV virus is and is not spread. If students are not involved in high-risk behaviors, then they have nothing to fear from interacting with people who are HIV positive.
3. Have a discussion led by the principal or school counselor on why it is important for the student body and community not to judge those with HIV. (How the student contracted the virus is irrelevant at this time.)
4. Answer any pertinent questions from the student body that will not be covered in homeroom.
5. Dismiss students to homeroom for related activity (see "**Student/Teacher Worksheet for First HIV Assembly**," page 141).

***Day Two***: **Student Assembly** – Attended by the whole student body, if possible.

1. Show *The Ryan White Story* video.
2. When the tape is over, send students back to their homerooms for an in-class activity with teachers (see "**Student/Teacher Worksheet for Second HIV Assembly**," page 142).

***Day Two***: **Staff Meeting** – After school.

1. Discuss any questions students asked that teachers were unable to answer.

2. Address concerns about safety procedures. Refer to district blood-borne infection policy and procedures.

3. Address concerns from staff about community reactions.

4. Discuss whether any further action needs to be taken. Will it be possible to return to a normal school day tomorrow?

## Community Activity

### *Day One*

It is suggested that the district's HIV Advisory Committee organize and facilitate a community meeting in the evening. The agenda for the meeting should allow time for the committee to do the following:

1. Clarify the situation.
2. Explain the school administration's major goals:
   - Prevent another Ryan White situation.
   - Prevent and eliminate any hysteria.
   - Maintain a safe and stable school environment for all.
3. Clarify how HIV transmission occurs (health care professional).
4. Clarify district's blood-borne infection policy.
5. Talk about importance of positive and supportive approach to HIV-positive students and their families.
6. Open the floor to questions for the HIV Advisory Committee.
7. Invite parents to attend the showing of *The Ryan White Story* video the following evening.

### *Day Two*

1. Welcome parents.
2. Show *The Ryan White Story* video.
3. Open the floor to questions for the HIV Advisory Committee.
4. Stress the need to support the HIV-positive student and his or her family.

## Alternate Plan for Day Two

This plan may be used if the school is unable to obtain a copy of *The Ryan White Story* video, which can be shown in the classroom, thus eliminating the need for a second student assembly.

***Directions:*** The teacher is to read the following story to the class and then *discuss* the questions that follow. *A transparency of this story on an overhead projector may be very helpful for students to refer to during the discussion.*

"William has AIDS. He has Kaposi's Sarcoma, and some of the purplish blotches from the disease have started to show on his face. He has come to a public swimming pool and paid

*continued on next page* ▶

CRISIS 4

the admission fee. As people are lined up after their shower to enter the pool, the lifeguard recognizes the blotches on William's face as a sign of AIDS. As a result, the lifeguard refuses to let William into the pool area. William refuses to get out of line and prevents others from getting into the pool area. You are behind William in line and want to go swimming. You become increasingly impatient. Some people in line start yelling at the lifeguard. Others yell at William."

1. If you were in line behind William, what would you do?

2. What do you think would have been the best thing for William to do in this situation?

3. What should the lifeguard have done in this situation?

4. Should people with HIV/AIDS be allowed in public swimming pools?

5. If you were the pool recreation director, what kind of policy do you think you might set for situations like this?

NOTE: Make use of the **Crisis Response Checklist** (see page 120), the **Student/Teacher Worksheet for First HIV Assembly** (see page 141), and the **Student/Teacher Worksheet for Second HIV Assembly** (see page 142) as you plan for this crisis.

# CRISIS 5

# Staff Death Due to Accident or Illness

Upon being informed of the death of a staff member due to an accident or illness, the Crisis Response Team should meet and use the **Crisis Response Checklist** (see page 120) as the planning begins. Although this may not be a complete list for all particular situations, the format will help to begin the process.

## Staff Meeting

The principal and school counselor, co-leaders of the Crisis Response Team, should call a staff meeting before the students report for school the next day. When scheduling the staff meeting, they should set aside time to do the following tasks:

1. Allow the staff to express grief and offer support to one another.
2. Introduce the Crisis Response Team:
   - Explain the roles of Crisis Response Team members.
   - Provide a written statement for teachers to read to students. Staff should be free to use other acceptable statements as long as they are sensitive to the situation.
   - Answer questions on procedures.
   - Identify Crisis Room locations.
3. Field questions from staff about how to answer student questions. (The psychologist or social worker serving as an advisor to the Crisis Response Team may lead this discussion.)
4. Make closing comments. Before the staff leaves, they need to be assured that:
   - Help is available to them as well as the students.
   - They are the key to maintaining a safe environment.
   - The information they have regarding the crisis is accurate.
   - The Roamers in the halls can help get students from classrooms to the Crisis Room and are trained to provide assistance in several ways.

# Statement for Teachers to Read

The following is a sample announcement teachers may read to their classes after a death of a staff member.

> **NOTE:** Family Liaison needs to have permission from the family to announce the death at school.

"We are sad to learn that ____(name)____, who __(job function)__, died as a result of (type of accident or illness)__ last night. We do not have any more information at this time . . .

(Or)

We are sad to learn that ____(name)____, who __(job function)__, died as a result of (type of accident or illness)__ last night. ____(family liaison)____ has talked with the family and this is the information we have at this time.

As more information becomes available, such as funeral arrangements and memorial services, we will pass it on to you. We will be passing out a form titled the **Personal Resource Survey**. Please take a few minutes to fill it out. Counselors will be available in a special support room that is for anyone who would like to talk about his or her feelings. Would anyone like to talk about any feelings he or she may be experiencing right now?"

# Sample Letter to Parents

The following is a sample letter the school can mail to students' parents after a staff member's death by accident or illness. It is strongly suggested that before this letter is mailed, *all facts are verified and permission to announce the staff member's death has been granted by the family of the deceased.*

Dear Parents,

We are very sad to announce that ____(name)____ of our teaching staff died yesterday as a result of ___(type of accident or illness)___. When a teacher dies, students go through many fears and adjustments. They also may begin to worry about the possibility of something happening to their own parents.

This is an important time for you to speak to your children. Often families use a time like this to reinforce their own personal spiritual values. It is also important to reassure your children that you are okay and that you are taking good care of yourself. Also, your children need to know that you have planned for someone to give them a place to live and care for them, in case something should ever happen to you. We talked with our students today and encouraged them to talk with you if they have any questions or concerns. We also let them know that there are people at school who care about them and are willing to listen. Please feel free to call if there is any other way we can be of assistance.

Sincerely,

_____

(Principal)

# Handling the Deceased's Classes

One of the main areas of concern following a teacher's death is how to deal with the teacher's classes.

> **NOTE:** It is important that someone the students know and trust, such as another teacher, administrator, counselor, coach or social worker, meets with them at the regular scheduled time. A substitute teacher with whom the children are not familiar should not be placed in the classroom during the critical period following a teacher's death.

Students will have questions and will be much more accepting of a familiar face. The following will also help during this transition period:

- Place a person on the staff who is trusted and well liked by the students as the initial substitute in the deceased's class. This person can be another teacher, administrator, counselor, coach or social worker.
- Make the transition to a permanent replacement when the critical period is over. Ease this person into relationships with the students by having them work playground duty, eating lunch with the students or engage in some other student-based activity.
- Train the permanent replacement teacher on potential problems and how to deal with them before he or she enters the classroom setting.

  Administrators and the replacement teacher should maintain communication with students' parents for help in identifying and assisting with problems.

The following may be useful for the classroom teacher in helping students recognize a loss and deal with grief. Although a classroom teacher may not use all of these activities, it is imperative that something be done to recognize the loss and help the students grieve so they can move on with a sense of closure.

- Write a condolence letter individually or as a group. This may provide an opportunity to say things that students feel should have been said when the person was alive.
- Have a discussion about the deceased and the grieving process.
- Create a book of poems or stories about the person who died.
- Make individual cards for the deceased's family.
- Draw pictures of memories of the deceased or comforting feelings.
- Encourage students to express their feelings to the family of the deceased. The classroom teacher can brainstorm with the class about what to say. If students cannot find the words, suggest a heartfelt "I am sorry." Also, showing up at the funeral is a statement that someone cares.
- Incorporate a Death Education unit as part of the regular education program, preferably *before* a tragedy occurs. Death Education can help take the mystery out of death and create an appreciation for life and the people we love.

# Media Interviews

The following list of suggestions can help the school provide accurate information to the media. This will help minimize the potential for inaccurate reporting, which will help avoid furthering the hurt felt by grieving family and friends.

> **NOTE**: The Media Liaison will need to work in tandem with the Family Liaison to determine what information has been approved by the family to be shared with the media.

- Set policies about dealing with the media before a tragedy occurs.
- Direct all media inquiries to the Media Liaison of the Crisis Response Team. This will avoid confusion in times of crisis and guarantee that accurate information is provided to the media.
- Be proactive with the media. Initiate contact with a phone call or press release.
- Use clear, simple language that readers and viewers can easily understand.
- Be polite, professional and courteous to the interviewer.
- Remember that the media has a job to do. View media coverage as an asset to the Crisis Response Team's work.
- Back up facts with original resources. Do not give erroneous information or speculate.
- Make it clear before being taped or recorded that discussion of the details about the cause of death is not appropriate.
- Avoid sensational or romantic statements.
- Only provide information that the deceased's family has approved to be made public.
- Do not allow the media to roam the school grounds, interviewing anyone they please. Establish clear ground rules when media are on campus.

## Memorials for Death By Accident or Illness

There are many differences associated with handling death from an accident or illness versus death by suicide. The difference between the two should be carefully considered and understood by the Crisis Response Team. The following is a list of actions that a school should consider in the case of death due to an accident or illness. Please note the differences between these procedures and those identified in the section titled "*Crisis 6: Staff Death By Suicide.*"

- Provide a moment of silence in the deceased's honor.
- Fly flags at half-mast.
- Encourage students or faculty to memorialize the deceased if they so desire. Their plan should be approved by the Crisis Response Team.
- Encourage memorials to celebrate the deceased's interests in life.
- Plant a shrub or tree on school grounds in remembrance of the deceased.
- With adult supervision, students may make "Treasure Box Memorials." Students write letters, poetry, or songs about the deceased to be presented to the family.

*continued on next page* ▶

**CRISIS 5**

- Make a collage of the staff member using photos and memorabilia from their days on campus and present it to the family.
- With adult supervision, students may design a T-shirt using sketches, photos, etc. in memory of the staff member. Proceeds from the shirt might go to a memorial scholarship fund or to a charity in their honor.
- Memorialize the staff member in the yearbook.
- Enlist groups, such as athletic teams, band or student government, to collect donations for flowers, scholarships or organizations in memory of the deceased.
- Encourage discussion on the cause of death.

## Returning Personal Property

The deceased staff member will likely have left items in his or her desk or locker that the family will want to have. The Family Liaison and one of the deceased's favorite co-workers should arrange to return the items to the family's home. These items should be returned after the funeral, unless they are of significant value.

The visit will likely be appreciated by family members. They may be very emotional and wish to visit for a while as they sort through the items and share their thoughts and feelings. It is important for school representatives to be especially sympathetic and compassionate at this time.

NOTE: Please make use of the **Crisis Response Checklist** (see page 120) and the **Student Personal Resource Survey** (see page 133) as you plan for this crisis.

# CRISIS 6

## Staff Death By Suicide

Upon being informed of the suicide of a teacher or staff member the Crisis Response Team should meet and use the Crisis Response Checklist (see page 120) as the planning begins. Although this may not be a complete list for all particular situations, the format will help to begin the process.

## Staff Meeting

The principal and school counselor, as co-leaders of the crisis response team, need to call a staff meeting before the students report for school the next day. When scheduling the staff meeting, they should set aside time to do the following tasks:

1. Allow the staff to express grief and offer support to one another.
2. Introduce the Crisis Response Team:
   - Explain the roles of Crisis Response Team members.
   - Provide a written statement for teachers to read to students. Staff should be free to use other acceptable statements as long as they are sensitive to the situation.
   - Answer questions on procedures.
   - Identify Crisis Room locations.
3. Field questions from staff about how to answer students' questions. (The psychologist or social worker serving as an advisor to the Crisis Response Team may lead this discussion.)
4. Make closing comments. Before staff leaves, they need to be assured that:
   - Help is available to them as well as the students.
   - They are the key to maintaining a safe environment.
   - The information they have regarding the crisis is accurate.
   - The Roamers in the halls can help get students from classrooms to the Crisis Room and are trained to provide assistance in several ways.

# Statement for Teachers to Read

The following is a sample announcement teachers may read to their classes after a suicide death of a staff member.

> **NOTE**: Family Liaison needs to have permission from the family to announce the death at school.

"As you all know by now, _____(name)_____ took his(her) life last evening. _____(name)_____ was a person who was really hurting inside. The action he(she) took was the result of this pain. This action is inappropriate. Let us not judge _____(name)_____ to be a bad person, but realize that there are more positive ways to handle our problems. We have all lost a friend and are hurting with you. When people take their lives, they hurt their families and friends too. Although we are sure _____(name)_____ never meant to hurt anyone, his(her) family and friends are now hurting. Let us understand that there are people who care about us and are willing to listen and help.

In handling your grief, I want you to understand the following points:

- We all have problems.
- Our problems do not last forever. Dark days will pass.
- Suicide is never a solution to our problems.

We will be handing out a form titled the **Student Personal Resource Survey**. Please take a few moments to fill it out. Counselors will be available in a special support room that is made available for anyone who would like to talk about his or her feelings. Thank you."

*(Or)*

"Yesterday afternoon, at approximately _____(time)_____, a tragedy occurred involving _(name)_. We all know that no one single incident or situation causes a person to commit suicide. We will never know all the reasons for _____(name)_____ actions. It is important to realize that we must reach out to each other at this time, be friends, listen, care and help each other understand, and realize that each one of us is important. In the days ahead, take time to tell one another that you care. We will be handing out a form titled the Personal Resource Survey. Please take a few moments to fill it out. Counselors will be available in a special support room that is for anyone who would like to talk about his or her feelings. Thank you."

After reading one of the provided statements, allow students to discuss the tragedy if they wish. As they talk, keep the following in mind:

- Encourage them to express their feelings.
- Try not to let the discussion glamorize the act.
- No one person is responsible.
- Reinforce that suicide is a tragedy. Do not allow someone to become larger in death than they were in life.
- Suicide does not solve problems. It creates them. Suicide is a never a solution to our problems.
- Take special note of students who appear unusually upset by this discussion. Make referrals if necessary.

© National Center For Youth Issues • www.ncyi.org • 1-800-477-8277
Please refer to page 2 for duplication information

# Sample Letter to Parents

The following is a sample letter the school can mail to students' parents after a suicide death of a staff member. It is strongly suggested that before this letter is mailed, *that all facts are verified and permission to announce the staff member's death has been granted by the family of the deceased.*

---

Dear Parents,

We are very sad to announce that\_\_\_\_\_(name)\_\_\_\_\_ took his(her) life on \_\_\_\_\_(date)\_\_\_\_\_. Suicide is always a very tragic and traumatic event in the school community. We are aware that grief due to suicide is different from grief due to death from natural causes.

Our Crisis Response Plan has been activated to maintain a safe and calm environment at school. Our emphasis at school will be to assist our students and staff in expressing their grief appropriately and to educate them in the area of suicide prevention. The staff has classroom discussion activities designed to accomplish these goals. Our counseling staff and the Crisis Response Team will also be available for assistance. We will do our best to help our students express their emotions and encourage them to be kind to themselves. We are on the alert for possible copycat behaviors and will arrange for these individuals to receive assistance.

As a parent, we encourage you to talk with your children about this tragedy. Allow them to express their feelings and concerns. Reaffirm your love for them and reassure them that you are willing to listen to their fears and problems.

Please feel free to call me if we can be of more assistance.

Sincerely,

\_\_\_\_\_(Principal)\_\_\_\_\_

---

# Handling the Deceased's Class

One of the main areas of concern following a teacher's death is how to deal with the teacher's classes. It is important that someone the students know and trust, such as another teacher, administrator, counselor, coach or social worker, meets with them at the regular scheduled time. A substitute teacher with whom the children are not familiar should not be placed in the classroom during the critical period following a teacher's death. Students will have questions and will be much more accepting of a familiar face. The following will also help during this transition period:

- Place a person on the staff who is trusted and well liked by the students as the initial substitute in the deceased's class. This person can be another teacher, administrator, counselor, coach or social worker.

- Make the transition to a permanent replacement when the critical period is over. Ease this person into relationships with the students by having them work playground duty, eating lunch with the students or engage in some other student-based activity.

- Train the permanent replacement teacher on potential problems and how to deal with them before he or she enters the classroom setting.

- Administrators and the replacement teacher should maintain communication with students' parents for help in identifying and assisting with problems.

The following may be useful for the classroom teacher in helping students recognize a loss and deal with grief. Although a classroom teacher may not use all of these activities, it is imperative that something be done to recognize the loss and help the students grieve so they can move on with a sense of closure.

- Write a condolence letter individually or as a group. This may provide an opportunity to say things that students feel should have been said when the person was alive.

- Have a discussion about the deceased and the grieving process.

- Create a book of poems or stories about the person who died.

- Make individual cards for the deceased's family.

- Draw pictures of memories of the deceased or comforting feelings.

- Encourage students to express their feelings to the family of the deceased. The classroom teacher can brainstorm with the class about what to say. If students cannot find the words, suggest a heartfelt "I am sorry." Also, showing up at the funeral is a statement that someone cares.

- Incorporate a Death Education unit as part of the regular education program, preferably before a tragedy occurs. Death Education can help take the mystery out of death and create an appreciation for life and the people we love.

# Media Interviews

The following list of suggestions can help the school provide accurate information to the media. This will help minimize the potential for inaccurate reporting, which will help avoid further hurt to grieving family and friends.

> **NOTE:** The Media Liaison will need to work in tandem with the Family Liaison to determine what information has been approved by the family to be shared with the media.

- Set policies about dealing with the media before a tragedy occurs.
- Direct all media inquiries to the Media Liaison of the Crisis Response Team. This will avoid confusion in times of crisis and guarantee that accurate information is provided to the media.
- Be proactive with the media. Initiate contact with a phone call or press release.
- Use clear, simple language that readers and viewers can easily understand.
- Be polite, professional and courteous to the interviewer.
- Remember that the media has a job to do. View the media coverage as an asset to the Crisis Response Team's work.
- Back up facts with original resources. Do not give erroneous information or speculate.
- Make it clear before being taped or recorded that discussion of the details of the cause of death is not appropriate.
- Avoid sensational or romantic statements.
- Only provide information that the deceased's family has approved to be made public.
- Do not allow the media to roam the school grounds, interviewing anyone they please. Establish clear ground rules when media are on campus.

# Memorial for Staff Death by Suicide

There are many differences associated with handling a death from suicide versus death from other causes. These differences should be carefully considered and understood by the Crisis Response Team. The following is a list of actions that your Crisis Response Team should consider.

> **NOTE:** These suggestions differ greatly compared to the memorial procedures identified in the "*Crisis 1*: Student Death Due To An Accident Or Illness." This is to avoid glamorizing suicide in any and every way.

- Do not announce the death over the P. A. System or conduct a moment of silence.
- Do not lower flags to half-mast.
- Avoid school-sanctioned tributes, memorials or events.
- Close friends who wish to remember the deceased in a special way should be encouraged to do so in a quiet way that celebrates life (e.g., purchase of a video on suicide prevention, a researched publication of a list of teen resources, etc.).

In the handling of death by suicide, the Crisis Response Team may need to explain these procedures, in order to discourage memorializing, glamorizing, romanticizing or in any way encouraging suicidal behavior.

# Returning Personal Property

The deceased staff member will likely have left items in his or her desk or locker that the family will want to have. The Family Liaison and one of the deceased's favorite co-workers should arrange to return the items to the family's home. These items should be returned after the funeral, unless they are of significant value.

The visit will likely be appreciated by family members. They may be very emotional and wish to visit for a while as they sort through the items and share their thoughts and feelings. It is important for school representatives to be especially sympathetic and compassionate at this time.

NOTE: Please make use of the **Crisis Response Checklist** (see page 120) and the **Student Personal Resource Survey** (see page 133) as you plan for this crisis.

© National Center For Youth Issues • www.ncyi.org • 1-800-477-8277
Please refer to page 2 for duplication information

# CRISIS 7

# Catastrophic Death Involving Several Students and/or Staff Members

The catastrophic death of several people can paralyze the entire school community. Many types of catastrophes can occur, such as:

- An automobile accident with several students involved.
- A school bus accident.
- A fire or natural disaster.

## Catastrophic Versus Single Incident Deaths

In a catastrophic situation, the entire school family will most likely be impacted. The school will need outlets for dealing with fear, hysteria and proper expression of grief. Therefore, it will be essential to the health and safety of the school to implement your Crisis Response Plan immediately. Crisis Rooms and classroom education will likely need to be implemented for a longer period of time. Community resources must be available to assist the Crisis Response Team, provide support for staff and help staff provide support for students. If the crisis is large scale (such as a school bus accident) the school will need to take actions that include the entire community.

Upon being informed of the catastrophic death of several students or staff members, the Crisis Response Team should meet and use the **Crisis Response Checklist** (see page 120) as a guide. Although this may not be a complete list for all particular situations, the format will help to begin the process.

## Staff Meeting

The principal and school counselor, as co-leaders of the Crisis Response Team, need to call a staff meeting before the students report for school the next day. When scheduling the staff meeting, they should set aside time to do the following tasks:

1. Allow the staff to express grief and offer support to one another.
2. Introduce the Crisis Response Team:
   - Explain the roles of Crisis Response Team members.
   - Provide a written statement for teachers to read to students. Staff should be free to use other acceptable statements as long as they are sensitive to the situation.
   - Answer questions on procedures.
   - Identify Crisis Room locations.
3. Field questions from staff about how to answer student questions. (The psychologist or social worker serving as an advisor to the Crisis Response Team may lead this discussion.)
4. Make closing comments. Before staff leaves the meeting, they need to be assured that:
   - Help is available to them as well as the students.
   - They are the key to maintaining a safe environment.
   - The information they have regarding the crisis is accurate.
   - The Roamers in the halls can help get students from classrooms to the Crisis Room and are trained to provide assistance in several ways.

An assembly should be scheduled after the initial announcement to inform the students of the procedures that will be implemented during the week. A few key individuals, such as the principal, counselor or favorite teachers, should speak about the tragedy and the need for grieving. Students should be dismissed to their homeroom to participate in grief expression activities. It is suggested that school be dismissed early the first day.

## Handling Classes In the Case of Multiple Staff Deaths

In the event of a catastrophic tragedy involving the death of more than one staff member, choosing multiple substitute/interim teachers will be necessary. The following are guidelines to help in such an instance.

1. If possible, substitutes should be well known by the students.
2. Get input on available substitutes from local teacher colleges.
3. Hold a debriefing and informational session for the substitutes.
4. Have a Roamer from the Crisis Team monitor classrooms where substitutes are teaching.
5. Make sure substitutes are aware of and follow the procedure for sending a student to the Crisis Room.
6. Crisis Team members need to be available to assist the substitute in any way possible.

© National Center For Youth Issues • www.ncyi.org • 1-800-477-8277
Please refer to page 2 for duplication information

# Action Plans

The following suggested activities, which may be altered to fit specific situations, are aimed at helping the school administration handle the major concerns of the students, staff and community. It is suggested that these action plans be implemented as soon as possible with a great degree of compassion.

## Staff and Student Body

*Emergency Staff Meeting* – Before students arrive for school.

1. Explain the plan of action to staff.
2. Answer any pertinent questions.
3. Adjust time schedules due to student assembly.
4. Review the worksheet and directions for teachers to use in homeroom following the assembly.
5. Outline procedures for dismissing classes from homeroom for abbreviated school day.

*Student Assembly* – Attended by the whole student body, if possible.

1. Clarify the situation.
2. Make presentations by the principal, school counselor (or popular teacher) and minister (all of whom should speak briefly, expressing their inability to understand why such tragedies occur). This will help students who are in shock over the news to realize that others are also in a state of disbelief. The principal should announce the availability and location of the Crisis Room for students who wish to talk about their feelings.
3. Dismiss students to homeroom for related activity (see Student/Teacher Activities After Assembly, next section).

## Student/Teacher Activities After Assembly

This program is for discussion purposes. It is recommended that these activities be completed together in class through oral discussion, not individually by students.

1. Have the students discuss how they feel.
2. Allow students time to gather with their friends in the classroom to share emotions and talk.
3. Discuss ways the school can remember the people involved in the tragedy.

## Community Activity

The next day following a catastrophe, the Crisis Response Team and school administration should organize and facilitate a community meeting in the evening. The agenda for the meeting should allow time to do the following:

*continued on next page* ▶

1. Clarify the situation.
2. Explain the school administration's major goals:
   - Implement a plan to help students deal with grief.
   - Prevent and eliminate fear and hysteria.
   - Maintain a safe and stable school environment.
3. Explain the grief process to parents and answer questions about how to talk to children.
4. Announce possible memorial plans. Accept ideas from the audience.
5. Answer other questions from the audience.

## Statement for Teachers to Read

The following is a sample announcement teachers may read to their classes after the death of staff and/or student.

> **NOTE:** Family Liaison needs to have permission from the family to announce the death at school.

"We are sad to learn that _____(names)_____ were killed last night. We do not have any more information at this time . . .

(Or)

We are sad to learn that _____(names)_____ were killed last night. _(family liaison)_ has talked with the families and this is the information we have at this time.

As more information becomes available, such as funeral arrangements and memorial services, we will pass it on to you. We will be passing out a form titled the Personal Resource Survey. Please take a few minutes to fill it out. Counselors will be available in a special support room that is for anyone who would like to talk about his or her feelings. Would anyone like to talk about any feelings he or she may be experiencing right now?"

© National Center For Youth Issues • www.ncyi.org • 1-800-477-8277
Please refer to page 2 for duplication information

# Sample Letter to Parents

Dear Parents,

We were very sad to hear that _____(names)_____ , died yesterday as a result of _____.
_____(name)_____ is the son/ daughter of _____(parents)_____ of _____(address)_____.
___(name)___ is the son/ daughter of ____(parents)____ of _____(address)_____.

The school's Crisis Response Team has met and discussed a set of planned procedures that have taken or will take place to help our students work through their grief. Counselors and professionals, as well as a trained Crisis Response Team and a caring staff, will be available to students.

Visitation:          _____(name)_____       _____(name)_____

Smith Funeral Home          Cole Funeral Home
Monday, January 5, 1998      Monday, January 5, 1998
2:00 to 5:00 p.m.            5:00 to 9:00 p.m.

Funeral Service:       _____(name)_____     _____(name)_____

St. Johns Lutheran Church    First Assembly Church
Tuesday, January 6, 1998      Wednesday, January 6, 1998
11:00 a.m.               1:00 p.m.

The _____(name)_____ and_____(name)_____ families have invited students to attend the funeral services. Students will be excused from school to do so with parent permission on the signed slip below.

We are also planning a community meeting on____(date/time)____ at____(location)____ to discuss the impact of this tragedy on our children. You are encouraged to attend.

Sincerely,


(Principal)

- - - - - - - - - - - - - - - - - - - - - - - - - - - - - - - - - - - - - - - - - - - - - - - - - - - - - - - - - - - - - - - - - - - -

I, _____, the parent of_____

❑     DO give my permission for my child to attend the funeral service

❑     DO NOT give my permission for my child to attend the funeral service

for _____on _____at_____.

Signed _____(parent/legal guardian)_____

# Memorial for Deaths Due to Catastrophe

There are a few differences associated with handling a death by catastrophe and other types of death. Fear, anxiety and hysteria may be more wide spread in the catastrophic death, because more students, friends and relatives are involved. Students may be feeling a great deal of confusion. These tremendous emotions often are overwhelming. The memorial service is often a difficult time for students and, therefore, members of the Crisis Response Team and school or area counselors should be available. Even though it may be a difficult time, memorials are encouraged to help survivors come to terms with the loss. The following is a list of actions for schools to consider in the event of multiple deaths due to a catastrophe.

- Provide a moment of silence in the deceased's honor.
- Fly flags at half-mast.
- Encourage students or faculty to memorialize the deceased if they so desire. (Their plan should be approved by the Crisis Response Team.)
- Encourage memorials to celebrate the deceased's interests in life.
- Plant shrubs or trees on school grounds in remembrance of the deceased.
- Memorialize them in a yearbook.
- Enlist groups, such as athletic teams, band or student government, to collect donations for flowers, scholarships or organizations in memory of the deceased.
- Encourage discussion on the cause of death.
- Get as many people involved as possible.

# Media Interviews

The following list of suggestions can help the school provide accurate information to the media. This will help minimize the potential for inaccurate reporting, which will help avoid further hurt to grieving family and friends.

> **NOTE:** The Media Liaison will need to work in tandem with the Family Liaison to determine what information has been approved by the family to be shared with the media.

- Set policies about dealing with the media <u>before</u> a tragedy occurs.
- Direct all media inquiries to the Media Liaison of the Crisis Response Team. This will avoid confusion in times of crisis and guarantee that accurate information is provided to the media.
- Be proactive with the media. Initiate contact with a phone call or press release.
- Use clear, simple language that readers and viewers can easily understand.
- Be polite, professional and courteous to the interviewer.
- Remember that the media has a job to do. View the media coverage as an asset to the Crisis Response Team's work.
- Back up facts with original resources. Do not give erroneous information or speculate.
- Make it clear before being taped or recorded that discussion of the details of the cause of the death is not appropriate.

CRISIS 7

- Avoid sensational or romantic statements.
- Only provide information that families of the deceased have approved to be made public.
- Do not allow the media to roam the school grounds, interviewing anyone they please. Establish clear ground rules when media are on campus.

## Dealing With the Siblings of the Deceased

1. Debrief the student before they come back to school following the incident.
2. Have a plan in place to offer support to the student in the event that he or she becomes overwhelmed by grief during the school day. Discussing this support plan with the student **before** there is an upset will help them feel more comfortable and secure.
3. Don't draw attention to the student if he becomes overwhelmed by his grief.
4. Guide fellow classmates on how to be supportive and understanding before the student returns to school.
5. Keep communication open with the family and discuss any issues you might see in the student.

## Returning Personal Property

The deceased students and/or staff will likely have left items in his or her desk or locker that the families will want to have. The Family Liaison and favorite teachers and fellow staff members should arrange to return the items to the families' homes. These items should be returned after the funeral, unless they are of significant value.

The visit will likely be appreciated by the families. They may be very emotional and wish to visit while they sort through the items and share their thoughts and feelings. It is important for school representatives to be especially sympathetic and compassionate at this time.

**NOTE:** Make use of the **Crisis Response Checklist** (see page 120), and the **Student Personal Resource Survey** (see page 133) as you plan for this crisis.

CRISIS 7

# Additional Situations and Scenarios

## Tragedy Occurring on Campus

Imagine this – classes are changing and a student collapses suddenly in the hallway and dies. Or, perhaps a student collapses in Physical Education class and cannot be revived. In cases such as these and others like them, you may wish to consider the following procedures. *Whatever procedures you develop, it is extremely important that every adult staff member in the building be aware of and follow the procedure established by the Crisis Response Team.*

- Send/call for help (main office, passers by, etc.).
- Call EMS.
- The staff is to help move all students into their next class.
- Crisis Team reports immediately to main office.
- All staff on prep period are to report to the main office. Be prepared to sub for Crisis Team members or help with other tasks.
- Locate siblings and walk them to the office. Do not leave them alone without an adult.
- Keep students in classrooms until student or staff member in crisis is removed from premises.
- A prepared statement will be delivered to classrooms to inform staff and students and supply discussion guidelines.
- Log all procedures taken in order to make an accurate report to the school district attorney. This log will help you evaluate your response and better respond to a situation such as this if it occurs in the future. It may also help a neighboring school district experiencing this same type of crisis.
- Have a staff informational meeting immediately after school.
- Put the crisis plan into motion.

As previously stated, every adult staff member in your school building needs to be aware of these steps in dealing with this particular crisis. Also, if siblings of the student in crisis are in the same building, we strongly recommend that an adult accompany the student to the office. Never leave this student alone without a responsible adult.

## Death of an Unpopular Student

One of the biggest mistakes the Crisis Response Team can make is underestimating the impact of the death of an unpopular student. An unpopular student may be defined as the school bully, a gang member, known drug dealer, etc. The response of the student body may be different, and may be something the Crisis Response Team cannot control. The school, however, must still show consistency in policy and procedure. If the school Crisis Response Team doesn't show consistency, they open themselves up for future problems. The death must be addressed, or the school can easily get into the "denial mode" which has plagued and continues to plague numbers of schools across the country.

This death still brings thoughts to the students' own mortality. The school must offer respect and talk about the gift of life. The Crisis Response Team strategy may not focus on the deceased student's life, but on our own individual mortality. The difference from a popular student dying may be as follows:

- Popular student – talk about *his* life.
- Unpopular student – talk about *our* lives.

The school can still make this situation a learning and growth experience.

## Tragedy During Summer Vacation

As our experience has taught us, tragedies involving students and staff don't always occur during the school year. How can the school Crisis Response Team respond when a tragedy occurs during summer vacation? The following list may be helpful in addressing the tragedy and providing comfort and assistance to the school family:

- Before school dismisses for the summer, make sure that the Crisis Response Team has the updated phone number and e-mail address of every staff member.
- If tragedy does occur, inform all team members via phone tree or e-mail.
- Make an "impact list" of students and staff the Team feels will be most impacted.
- The Family Liaison should make contact with the family of the deceased.
- Notify families of students and staff on the impact list.
- Open up the school auditorium for a few hours for students and staff to come and comfort and support each other.
- Put the incident on the agenda for the beginning of the school year staff meeting.
- Make appropriate referrals.

## School Bus Accident

A school bus involved in a serious accident has the potential to cause a great deal of pandemonium and confusion. Hopefully, the school will be able to identify the students riding the bus by the bus number. One of the initial actions by the school is to identify the students involved and what school building(s) they attend. We also suggest that a designated site be established in the plan ahead of time. A township hall is usually a better site than the actual school building. The following is a scenario that will give your team some structure as they think through this situation:

**Situation** – A school bus transporting middle school students to school in the morning is involved in a serious accident. The local police contacts the school to inform them of the location and probable severity:

- Attempt to locate list of student names that may be on the bus.
- Contact parents or guardians of students on bus and direct them to the local township hall where police and school officials will be available to share information.
- Keep middle school counselors at the middle school so familiar faces will be with the middle school students.

*continued on next page* ▶

- Assess if elementary and high school counselors will be needed at the township hall and who will be needed for support at the elementary and high schools.
- Locate siblings of students involved in bus accident. Follow the established procedure of the planning team.
- Put the tragedy component of the Crisis Response Plan in motion.
- Hold staff informational meeting as soon as possible.

The above list is certainly not a "one size fits all" approach. Hopefully, it can provide the Crisis Response Team with a foundation as to how to approach and build a plan to address this very difficult situation.

## Letters to Parents

In handling a tragedy in the school family, we strongly believe that communicating with all parents and guardians of the entire student body is of the greatest importance. There are samples of letters in this book that you may use to accomplish this task. How the letters get home to the parents or guardians will be your decision. If the Crisis Response Team feels the need to write their own letter, the following list of cautions should be considered:

- Start out with sensitivity – "we are sad to announce."
- Stress what the school is doing – "the Crisis Team has activated a plan," "Crisis Rooms are set up and staffed by counselors for students and staff who may need extra help", "Teachers have been trained and equipped with appropriate plans."
- Encourage parents to talk with their children and listen to their concerns.
- Offer details about funeral arrangements or memorial services and donations.
- Details about how the tragedy occurred usually are not appropriate.
- Encourage parents to call if the school can be of further assistance.

**NOTE:** The Family Liaison should make sure that the school has the family's permission to announce the death *__before__* the letter is created and sent home.

*We also strongly advise that the principal of the school write and send a condolence note to the family of the deceased. It is very comforting and encouraging to the family to be reminded that their school truly cares.*

# Memorial Services

A memorial service provides students and staff with an opportunity to share memories and respect for the grieving family and each other. Students and staff can acknowledge the loss, seek closure and begin the healing process. Memorial services can be long or short and take place indoors or outdoors on the school grounds, wherever is most appropriate. It may be scheduled the week of the death or at a later date. The deceased's family should be invited to attend.

It is important to get as many students involved in the memorial service as possible. The faculty member chosen to coordinate the service should give careful consideration to which students will read at the service. Look for students who are comfortable speaking in front of people, are respected by the student body, and are friends of the deceased. It is important that these services provide an opportunity for those who knew or were close to the deceased to become involved. The following recommendations for a memorial service can be altered to fit the need of your school. In addition to the suggested services in this section, a local community hospice may be able to provide additional suggestions and sample memorial service plans.

## Religious Service

Students should be directed to enter the place of service in a quiet and respectful way. Personal effects of the deceased should be displayed.

1. *Opening Song* – Taken from a liturgy song-book or other as desired.
2. *Opening Prayer* – A local clergy member or a student should say a short prayer. When selecting a student to lead the prayer, make sure he or she is respected and is a friend of the deceased.
3. *Speaker* – Frequently a clergy member from the deceased's church. Arrange for some time for the speaker to talk with close friends and teachers of the deceased before the service.
4. *Reading* – Select passages from scripture to be read by friends of the deceased. A number of appropriate scriptures are listed at the end of this section (see "Scripture Readings," page 81).
5. *Comments* – Short comments by students who were friends of the deceased. Teachers and staff may also wish to share uplifting or comforting thoughts.
6. *Closing Prayer* – Given by a member of the clergy, staff member or student.
7. *Closing Song* – Examples are provided at end of this section (see "Music Selections," page 80). After close, students are ushered out in a quiet and formal manner.

## Non-Religious Service

Non-religious services often take place in the school auditorium or gymnasium. Personal effects of the deceased should be displayed. A banner, made by students, can be hung in honor of the deceased. Students should be directed to enter the place of service in a quiet and respectful manner.

*continued on next page* ▶

1. Opening Song – May be a favorite song of deceased as long as it is appropriate.
2. Speakers – Principal or teacher can start by saying a few words.
3. Song – May be sung by a group, school choir, or played by the band. A student may also want to play an instrument or sing a solo.
4. Sharing – Close friends, teachers and staff members may wish to say a few words.
5. Final Words – The principal or another person may say a few final words about the deceased. Ask a family member to participate during the service.
6. Closing Song – Same options as the opening song. After close, students leave in a quiet and formal manner.

## Music Selections

The following is a list of music selections that could be used at school memorial services. This is not a complete list, and those in charge of the service are encouraged to add other appropriate selections, especially those that had special meaning to the deceased.

- Wind Beneath My Wings (Bette Midler)
- That's What Friends Are For (Dionne Warwick and Stevie Wonder)
- Whenever I Call You Friend (Kenny Loggins)
- Forever (Kenny Loggins)
- Friends (Michael and Deborah Smith)
- Lean On Me (Thelma Huston and the Winans)
- Amazing Grace (John Newton, Tune: Early American Melody)
- You Gave Me Love (Amy Grant)
- I Believe Words and Music (Ervin Drake, Irvin Graham, Jimmy Shirl, Al Stillman)
- Shepherd of My Heart (Sandi Patty)
- Father's Eyes (Amy Grant)
- For Everything There Is A Time (Donald J. Reagan, Glory and Praise, NALR)
- Treasure (Amy Grant, Gary Chapman)
- Love Will Find A Way (Amy Grant)
- Live Like You Were Dying (Tim McGraw)
- Three Wooden Crosses (George Strait)

## School Remembrance Activities

- Plant trees, shrubs or flowers in honor of the deceased.
- Stage a balloon release with memories of deceased written on attached cards.
- Make a memory quilt and display at school. Adult supervision is required.
- Create a scrapbook of special school memories of deceased.
- Dedicate a plaque or picture.
- Purchase a piece of equipment, audiovisual materials or books.

- Purchase Death Education materials in the deceased's name that focus on helping children cope with grief.
- Conduct an assembly or memorial service.
- Establish a memorial scholarship in name of deceased.

## Scripture Readings

The following are examples of popular scripture readings that may be used at school memorial services. Scriptures may be added and used to fit individual situations.

- Psalm 131 – We are assured that humble trust in the Lord brings us peace.
- Psalm 121 – We are assured that the Lord is our protector now and forever.
- Psalm 62 – We hear that God's love is constant.
- Romans 8:14 – Assures us that God welcomes all who follow Him.
- Isaiah 57: 18-19 – Reminds us that the creator promises to hear, lead, and comfort the mourner.
- Isaiah 12: 2 – Tells us that we need not be afraid, for God is with us.
- Isaiah 43: 1-3 – Assures us that no matter how greatly we are troubled, God will stay with us, and we will survive the pain.
- Ecclesiastes 3:1,2,4,6 – We are told there is a time for everything, even a time to grieve and cry.
- Psalm 23 – Assures us of God's ever presence with us, and the courage He gives us to overcome our fears.

# Suicide Education and Prevention

This section centers on education and prevention of crisis-related issues, including grief management and the facts about suicide. It contains ideas, suggestions, and activities to help children overcome grief and loss. You will also find helpful information about the intervention process when dealing with a potentially suicidal person.

# Grief Management

In helping students deal with the loss of a friend, classmate or staff member, it is important for the Crisis Response Team and entire staff to have a basic understanding of grief and associated feelings. Grief can be defined in terms of deep sorrow and pain that causes distress. Common synonyms for grief include trouble, tribulation, mourning, regret, affliction and sadness. In his book *Concerning Death: A Practical Guide For Living*, Earl Grollman, a Jewish Rabbi, defines grief as "the intense emotion that floods life when a person's inner security system is shattered by an acute loss, usually associated with the death of someone significant in his or her life."[3] Saint Augustine suggested that grief is a strange mixture of joy and sorrow: "Joy to be yet alive, and sorrow to have life diminished by the loss of one we love."

Grief is composed of adjustments, apprehensions, and uncertainties that strike life, making it difficult to organize and direct energy. Because part of the lives of students who experience a loss will have been spent interacting with the deceased, they will not only grieve for the deceased and the deceased's family, but also for their own sense of loss. They will likely feel that the person has been taken away from them.

## The Grief Cycle

The following is a list of behavioral characteristics students may feel and exhibit as a result of a death of a family member, friend or staff member. Students may experience all or just a few of the following:

- *Numbness* – This is a very common reaction when learning of the death of a friend or loved one. It often accompanies the belief that what has happened is not real and likely the mind's way of cushioning itself from the full emotional impact of the loss. This feeling of numbness will slowly give way to other grief-related feelings.

- *Disbelief and illusions* – As the numbness wears off, people will go through periods of intermittent disbelief. Survivors may act as if the deceased is still alive. They may dream of the deceased and find it hard to believe that the deceased is not returning.

- *Time of inner conflict* – Grieving students often become restless, experience appetite loss or have trouble sleeping. The inner conflict they experience can result in lowered energy levels. These feelings come about as students hold to memories of the deceased and try to keep up familiar routines, which serve as reminders of their loss. On one hand they feel guilty for still being alive, while on the other they may feel as though they are betraying the deceased if they turn away from the familiar.

- *Guilt* – This is often one of the first emotions to be experienced and one of the last with which to be dealt. Young students may believe that their destructive wishes caused the death of their parent, teacher or fellow classmate. Older students are more likely to realize that their wishes did not cause the death, but still may feel guilt from a previous disagreement or incident with the deceased that could have been handled better.

- *Anger* – Although it often goes unrecognized, grieving students and adults alike will be angered over a loss. It is not easy to admit to feeling resentment toward the deceased, but on a deep level, most individuals do. Survivors may believe that the deceased friend or

*continued on next page* ▶

3.  Grollman, E. (1974). *Death: A practical guide for living*. Beacon Press.

relative has rejected and abandoned them and, in dying, has caused confusion and problems. When a parent dies, young children experience anger because they believe their survival is at stake and blame the parent for deserting them. This combination of guilt and anger is also common among older students and adults. Because it is considered taboo by some to speak negatively of deceased people, feelings of anger are usually focused inward or expressed indirectly.

## Proper Grief

"What is the proper way to grieve?" In helping students express their grief, teachers need to recognize that there is no universal or absolute answer to this question. Grief is primarily an individual experience, and, as such, rarely will two people grieve alike. In most cases, the proper way to grieve is to do what comes naturally. Crisis Team members and teachers must recognize that grieving is a necessary process one must go through so healing can take place.

Numerous studies have indicated that improper grieving can be hazardous to one's health. Therefore, a distinction between normal and abnormal grief must be made. In normal grief, individuals are able to work their way back to a healthy frame of mind and a productive lifestyle. Abnormal grief is characterized by a chronic state of psychological or physical symptoms.

Following a death, it is sometimes difficult to distinguish between normal and abnormal grief. Abnormal grief often shows up in extreme behaviors. For example, it is normal for people to show their emotions while they grieve. It is abnormal for people to react coldly, or in contrast, fall to pieces for long periods of time.

## Needs of the Bereaved

General concepts to consider when dealing with grieving individuals include the following:

- They need understanding and comfort in dealing with their loss.
- Those whose loss was sudden will differ from those who lose someone to a prolonged illness.
- The greatest time of need for friends and relatives of the terminally ill is while the person is dying.
- The grief period for people who experience a sudden loss usually lasts much longer than the grief over an extended illness. The real impact of the grief may surface months after the event. By then, there is a danger that friends have stopped visiting or have grown too impatient to listen.
- Those who refuse to come to terms with their loss may grieve for years.
- Both excessive grief and lack of grief are abnormal.
- The average length of the grief cycle is 24 months.

## The School's Role in Grief Management

Thousands of school age children die each year and thousands more experience the death of a parent, sibling or grandparent. It is estimated that one in every seven children loses someone close to them to death before the child reaches the age of 10.

Helping children deal with the death of a loved one is a very difficult problem in our culture. In many situations, their questions and feelings are ignored. Communication about death is easier when children feel they have permission to talk about the subject and believe that others really care about their views and are interested in their questions.

Classrooms, for many children, serve as secondary, or even substitute, families. The role of the classroom may be especially important when parents are deep in grief and are unable to provide children with the attention they need. In these cases, children lose not only the person who died, but in a sense, their surviving parents as well. School personnel are frequently willing to assume the parental role, but most feel insecure about the possibility of saying the wrong thing.

**A school's goal in dealing with a death should be to:**

1. Acknowledge the death honestly.
2. Allow students and staff to express their feelings.
3. Offer an outlet for the students and staff who desire to help.

It is very important that school personnel realize that grieving takes a prolonged period of time. They should also be especially sensitive to special times of the year such as holidays, birthdays and other special events that are supposed to be happy times in the life of the child. These special times often rekindle memories of the deceased and feelings of loss and sadness.

## Grief and Loss With Students: Suggestions for Teachers

Many times during an educator's career, there will be students in the school or classroom who are grieving over a significant loss. Educators experience great frustration in not knowing what to do when confronted with a grieving student. That is why it is essential for schools to provide an environment that is conducive to helping a student work through the fears, anger, confusion and frustration that accompany grief. This is a very crucial time in the student's life. The following suggestions may help in working with grieving students:

- Returning to school after the loss of a loved one is an important first step for a grieving student. It signals a return (or an attempt to return) to a normal life. Provide structure and expectations regarding school work, but be flexible with regard to time for assignments to be completed.
- The first day back, help the student become settled. Inquire how the student is doing and maintain an open line of communication, while making sure the student does not feel isolated from others. Do not pressure the student to talk, but let the student know that you care and are available to listen and help.
- Act as naturally as possible.
- You may help the student open up by calmly sharing your personal feelings about their loss. Always be honest and sympathetic.
- It is okay to shed a few tears with the grieving student.
- Avoid confusing phrases such as "went away," "expired" or "went to sleep." Use the correct language (i.e., death, died, dead) with sensitivity.
- Listen and accept. Let students tell you what is bothering or is personally important to them.

*continued on next page*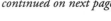

- Be alert for uncharacteristic behaviors related to their grief, such as truancy, lack of interest in school, anger toward classmates, teachers or administrators, or physical manifestations.
- Allow the student to talk about the loss as much as needed.
- Do not impose personal religious beliefs.
- Do not be afraid to make mistakes. An error in judgment will not destroy a grieving student.
- Prolonged or abnormal grief behavior may signal a need to make a referral to the counseling department or a meeting with the student's parents.
- Make sure the student knows that teachers care and are there to help.
- Remind students to talk with the school guidance counselor or persons staffing the Crisis Rooms.

**The following comments can help grieving children return to school after a death in the family:**[4]

- "I am sorry that ____(name)____ died." (Rather than "I am sorry about what happened.")
- "I cannot know how you feel, but I want to help you any way I can."
- "I care about you."
- "Let's talk about what might make you more comfortable in class."
- "You might want to keep a journal to help you express your feelings."
- "If you feel like sharing any of your writing with me, I would like to read it."
- "I can see that you are very sad."
- "I cannot know how you feel, but I also had a death in my family." (Briefly sharing a personal story will help build trust.)

### What *Not* To Do

- Avoid the student.
- Minimize the loss.
- Change the subject if the student brings up the deceased.
- Tell the student that the hurt will go away. No one knows how long the student's grief cycle will take.
- Tell the student "I know how you feel."
- Use clichés like, "We all have to die sometime," or "at least you knew it was coming," or "it definitely was God's will."

# Classroom Activities for Dealing With Grief

The following may be helpful for the classroom teacher in helping students recognize a loss and deal with grief. Although a teacher may not use all these activities, it is imperative that something be done to recognize the loss and help the students grieve so they can move on with a sense of closure.

- Write a condolence letter individually or as a group. This may provide an opportunity to say things that students feel should have been said when the person was alive.
- Have a discussion about the deceased and the grieving process.

4.  Mothers Against Drunk Driving. (1992) *Guidelines and suggestions when handling a loss.* Newsletter 2-3.

- Create a book of poems or stories about the person who died.
- Make individual cards for the deceased's family.
- Draw pictures of memories of the deceased or comforting feelings.
- Encourage students to express their feelings to the family of the deceased. The classroom teacher can brainstorm with the class about what to say. If students cannot find the words, suggest a heartfelt "I am sorry." Also, showing up at the funeral is a statement that you care.
- Incorporate a Death Education unit as part of the regular education program, preferably before a tragedy occurs. Death Education can help take the mystery out of death and create an appreciation for life and the people we love.

## Reintegrating a Student Into the Classroom Following Loss

The following guidelines can be helpful for a teacher to understand the grieving process. These guidelines should be reviewed after any death of a student, student's family member or staff.

- Before the student returns to school, have the class send a card expressing sympathy to the student and their family. This prevents each class member from having to express their personal condolences. Another option is to have each student make a separate card. Discuss what is appropriate to write. Screen cards before sending to make sure each one is appropriate. Remember, this is an opportunity to teach students about sensitivity towards someone who has experienced a significant loss.
- If at all possible, attend the visitation at the funeral home, funeral or memorial service. This sends a message of support to the student.
- Discuss the student's return with the class. Emphasize that the student has just experienced a great loss and will need a long time to adjust. Help the students think through how they will interact with the grieving student. Encourage them to be as normal as possible. Talk about helping the student feel like a part of the class, as he or she was before the tragedy. Help the student feel welcome, but do not make a big fuss. The student may or may not want to share personal feelings.
- When the student does return to class, welcome the student back and acknowledge the loss (e.g., "we are sorry about"). Then quickly help the student re-engage with the class.
- Let the student and the class know (through your actions) that life goes on. Carry on as usual.
- If the student emotionally breaks down, do not draw attention to him or her. When the class is involved in an activity that does not require teacher direction, quietly comfort the student. A warm touch and kindness can be of great assistance. The student should know the teacher is there to help in any way possible. Offer the child a private place within the school to gather his or her composure.
- Keep communication open with the family and discuss any issues you might see in the student.

# Suicide: Facts and Myths

Suicide currently ranks second behind accidents as the major cause of death for Americans aged 15 to 24.[1] Schools have been identified as one of the major areas of stress that may be associated with teen suicide. In being responsible for the health and safety of its staff and students, it is important that schools establish policies and procedures to maintain order and offer appropriate suicide prevention services. Strategies need to be in place so that intervention can occur with students and staff who pose a potential threat to their personal safety.

Suicide is usually not a result of one or a few isolated events in an individual's life, but the end of a series of extremely frustrating events. The leading means of committing suicide are (1) firearms (59%), (2) poisoning (19%), and (3) strangulation (14%).[1] The main *causes* of suicide, however, include:

- Alcohol or other drug addiction
- Break up of family relationships
- Depression
- Feelings of insecurity
- Illness
- Broken love affairs
- Economic or business affairs that turn sour
- Disfiguring injuries or disease

In many ways, suicide is a social act meant to influence others. It is one type of communication meant to say:

- "I am angry and I am going to punish you in the worst way possible. You will feel guilty long after I kill myself."
- "You never paid attention to me. No one has ever paid attention to me. But if I kill myself, you will have to pay attention to me."
- "I need help but I am not able to ask for it. I do not know how to ask for help. This is a way to ask for help."
- "The pain of my life is too great and I cannot stand it any longer. Either someone has to help me out of this pain or I will help myself out by dying."
- "I want to control you and I can do that by attempting suicide. I will be the victim and you will be the rescuer."

The above list, although not complete, gives an idea of what someone who is suicidal may be thinking. Being familiar with what and how a person thinks increases the effectiveness of dealing with that person. Again, suicide is *not* usually a result of a few isolated events in an individual's life, but the end result of many frustrating setbacks.

---

1.  National Center for Health Statistics (1997). Atlanta, GA. Centers for Disease Control and Prevention.

# Suicide Facts

The following suicide facts are based on official statistics published by the American Association of Suicidology.[8]

1. Currently, there are slightly more than 30,000 suicides annually. That is 83 suicides per day or one suicide every 17 minutes.

2. Rates of suicide are highest in the western regions, especially the mountain states.

3. Suicide is the eighth leading cause of death in the U.S.

4. Males commit suicide at rates three to four times that of females.

5. Firearms are the most often used method for suicide.

6. Suicide rates have traditionally decreased in times of wars and increased in times of economic crises.

7. Spring and Mondays consistently rank highest in number of suicides.

8. Suicide rates are highest among individuals who are divorced or widowed and lowest among those who are married.

9. With youth and young adults, ages 15 to 24, suicide rates increased more than 200% from the 1950s to the late 1970s. Current rates are approximately still 200% higher than the 1950s.

10. Suicide ranks second only to accidents as a cause of death among youth and young adults, ages 15 to 24.

11. Suicide rates among whites are approximately twice that of non-whites.

12. Native Americans have the highest suicide rates overall. There are large differences, however, between tribes.

13. The majority of those who are suicidal display clues and warning signs.

14. It is estimated that at least 3.5 million Americans have had a loved one who committed suicide.

15. 50% of teenagers who attempt suicide have a depressed, suicidal mother.

16. 50% of adolescents who attempt suicide describe their family life as "on-going warfare."

17. 80% of patients who are medically treated for major depression attempt suicide within the first three months of improvement.

18. 95% of teenagers who attempt suicide survive.

19. Depressed students are often over looked because they are considered troublemakers.

---

8.  Michigan Association of Suicidology. (1997).

# Common Myths About Teen Suicide[3,9,10]

*Myth*: Youth who talk about suicide rarely attempt it.
**Fact**: Most who attempt or commit suicide have given verbal clues.

*Myth*: Talking about suicide will make it happen.
**Fact**: Talking about suicide does not place ideas into young people's heads that are not already there. There is evidence that once a suicide occurs, others may follow as a contagious reaction to hopelessness.

*Myth*: The tendency towards suicide is inherited.
**Fact**: There is no evidence of a genetic link. A previous suicide in the family, however, may establish a destructive model for dealing with stress and depression.

*Myth*: Teenage suicides happen at night.
**Fact**: Most teenage suicides occur between 3:00 and 6:00 in the afternoon, presumably when the suicidal person can be seen and stopped.

*Myth*: Suicidal people leave notes.
**Fact**: Only a small number, approximately 15%, leave notes.

*Myth*: If a person wants to commit suicide, nothing can stop them.
**Fact**: Suicidal people have mixed feelings about death. They often send out messages and clues that point to their pain. No one is suicidal all the time. Many suicides can be prevented.

*Myth*: Youth who want to commit suicide are mentally ill.
**Fact**: Mental illness increases the risk of suicide. Most young people who attempt or commit suicide, however, would not be diagnosed as mentally ill. Youth suicide is often a sudden and urgent reaction to accumulative events and stress.

*Myth:* A teenager who has been suicidal is never out of danger.
**Fact:** Many youth who have been depressed recover and lead normal, healthy lives. They learn constructive, rather than destructive, ways to cope with feelings and disappointments.

3. Grollman, E. (1974). *Death: A practical guide for living. Beacon Press.*
9. Gordon, S. (1989). *When living hurts.*
10. Klagsbrun, F. (1984). *Too young to die.*

# Suicide Warning Signs

Behavioral clues that a suicidal person might exhibit include the following;

1. Previous threats or attempts at suicide.

2. Support for an important role model who committed suicide.

3. Feelings of being a failure.

4. Radical personality changes (e.g., persistent sadness, loss of interest in usual activities).

5. Withdrawal from family, friends and regular activities.

6. Noticeable changes in eating or sleeping habits.

7. Neglect in personal appearance.

8. A decline in the quality of school work.

9. Violent or rebellious behavior.

10. Drug or alcohol abuse.

11. Verbal hints (e.g., "I will not be a problem for you much longer," or "Nothing matters").

12. Giving away favorite possessions.

13. Suddenly becoming cheerful after a prolonged depression (which may indicate the decision to commit suicide has been made).

*If students or staff display some or all of the above behaviors, the following questions will help in further identifying the seriousness of the risk.*

- Has that person had a recent major loss of a loved one?

- Has there been a recent major disappointment or humiliation in this person's life?

- Has there been a sudden lack of communication between this person and teachers, friends or family?

- Is there evidence of an unstable home life?

- Does this person exhibit feelings of revenge against a former love interest, parent or another person?

Consider suicidal acts, however lethal, as being an effort to stop unbearable anguish or intolerable pain. Often, suicide can be prevented by letting others know about a person's struggles, breaking what could be a fatal secret, offering help, getting loved ones interested and responsive, creating action around the person at risk and showing the individual that someone loves and cares about them. It short, it is better to do something than nothing.

# Intervening With a Potentially Suicidal Person

The following guidelines should be followed when dealing with a person who is potentially suicidal:

1.  Be up front. Ask if the person is thinking about suicide. This might be the most single, reliable way to find out if the person is really thinking about suicide.

2.  If a person is thinking about suicide, find out how seriously. Do not be afraid to confront the person directly. Ask if the individual is thinking about carrying through with the suicide and how it will be done. Most people who have not thought about how they will commit suicide will be disturbed by the thought. If, however, the person explains how the suicide will take place, a crisis exists. Do not leave the person alone. Either stay with the individual or have someone else stay until a professional counselor or psychologist can intervene. If the suicidal individual is a student, parents should be notified immediately.

3.  If the suicidal individual is a student and his or her parents refuse to cooperate, inform them that not cooperating is considered child neglect, and a referral will immediately be made to Child Protective Services.

4.  An individual that does not have a plan but does admit to suicidal thoughts should be referred for counseling.

5.  Be a good listener. Listen not only to what the person is saying but also to what the person is **not** saying.

6.  Evaluate the individual. Does the person have a plan? Is the individual speaking in a rational way or just being emotional?

7.  Do not suggest that the individual carry through with the plan. What if the person heeded the advice? Reverse psychology is not a good approach with those contemplating suicide.

8.  Accept every feeling and complaint the person expresses. Do not argue with the individual and do not confirm suicide as an appropriate solution.

9.  Be aware of fast recoveries. The person may just feel better because he or she has talked about it and may feel relieved that the decision not to commit suicide has been made.

10. Be supportive and affirmative. Assure the individual that everything possible will be done to help.

11. Seek further consultation. Recognize your personal limitations.

12. Help the person realize that suicide is irreversible. A suicide cannot be undone. Suicide is a permanent solution to a temporary problem.

13. Remind the person that depressed feelings will pass. Help the person realize that there is someone who cares about him or her. Help the person also realize that he or she does have something to offer. (A depressed individual usually will not want to listen to clichés, like "when the going gets tough, the tough get going.")

14. Never leave the person alone in an acute crisis. If the person has made a plan and appears serious, either go get help together or leave the suicidal individual with someone else and go seek help.

# School Protocol for Dealing With a Student Threatening Suicide

A student threatening suicide, exhibiting self-destructive behaviors, or revealing suicidal thoughts through comments or writings must be taken seriously. It is to be assumed that this student could act out the threat. In addition to the guidelines presented in the previous section, the following should be implemented in the case where a student is threatening suicide:

1. Immediately notify the school principal, using the "**Suicidal Behavior Reporting Form**" (see page 135).

2. The principal should choose a person or persons to stay with the student during the crisis period and contact the student's parents. The principal should provide the parents with a description of the incident and an explanation of the school's concern. Certain qualified staff members should also be made available to communicate with the family.

3. The parents should be advised to pick up their child at school. The student should not be left alone until the parent(s) arrives. The parents should complete the "**Parental Agreement/Release Form**" (see page 137) when picking up their child.

4. If a parent cannot be reached, the principal should call community resources (e.g., county mental health, hospital psychiatric unit, the student's church minister).

5. The Crisis Response Team should be called on to provide assistance to staff, students and the suicidal student's family.

6. The Crisis Response Team should follow up the incident with a report to the Superintendent of Schools, using the "**Suicidal Behavior Reporting Form**" (see page 135), and have a copy of the report filed in a confidential file in the principal's office.

# Survivors of Suicide

## Grief Reactions of Suicide Survivors

When helping friends and classmates of a suicide victim, it is important to know which reactions to expect. The following reactions are normal ways of coping and part of the overall healing process:

- Shock – A sense of numbness or lack of feeling. The belief that what has happened is not real.

- Denial – Having a difficult time believing that a person is really dead even though they are aware of the reality.

- Guilt – Usually one of the first feelings to be experienced after suicide and one of the last to be dealt with. The survivors' guilt is relieved when they come to the realization that the suicide was the choice of the person who committed the act. We are not responsible for other people's actions.

- Emotional outburst and irritability – Survivors may experience outbursts of crying, anger, denial, guilt, shame, panic and fear. Because of stress, people may become more impatient, irritable and restless. All these may lead to disrupted sleep and eating patterns.

- Depression or sadness – After experiencing the above feelings over a period of time, survivors may become emotionally drained and depressed. This can last for weeks or months, with good days occasionally happening.

- Anger - Anger towards the deceased is common. Often this emotion is the result of people grieving for themselves, rather than for the deceased.

## Helping Survivors of Suicide

The following guidelines can be helpful for staff and students who want to help others struggling with a friend or loved one's suicide:

- Initiate conversation about the suicide and let the survivors know that their grief is different than if the death occurred through natural causes. Do not be afraid to use the word suicide. This helps to desensitize individuals and allow them to face the reality of what happened.

- Do not assume you know how they feel. Just listen patiently, without being judgmental.

- If survivors feel guilty, let them know that the death was not their fault. The individual made the choice to commit suicide.

- Provide them with information about suicide and grief. The school's Crisis Response Team should have information available.

- Do not let them feel that they are alone. Help them realize that others have gone through similar experiences and that they too will survive.

- Give them permission to be angry at the deceased, cry and experience all other emotions they may have.

- Let them know that this will be a very stressful time. Encourage them to be kind to themselves and to eat and sleep well.

- Do not try to answer the question if they ask "Why?" Survivors will ask this question over and over and may answer part of the question on their own. The question, however, can never be fully answered.
- Recognize that survivors are often angry at what happened and may take their anger out on staff. Try to be patient and understanding.
- Sometimes survivors become suicidal themselves. Watch for clues and do not be afraid to ask them how they feel and if they have thoughts of dying.
- Inform them that the grief process is a long one, lasting on average 24 months.

# Helping Children Cope With Grief

## Grief Tasks for Children

The following is a list of tasks that experts have found useful in working with children who are grieving over the loss of a loved one. Children need to accomplish these tasks if grief is to be dealt with successfully:

1. *Understanding* – Accepting that the loss has happened and is real. In her book About Dying, Sara Bonnett-Stein suggests that, "Until children are quite sure a person is no more, and never will be, they cannot finish the work of mourning. And if they cannot finish it, they cannot free themselves to go on with life and love and growing."[5]
2. *Grieving* – Working through the various stages of grief and mourning and helping others through various emotions, including anger, fear and confusion.
3. *Commemorating* – Formal or informal acts, celebrations, rituals or remembrances that mark the death or loss in an observable way.
4. *Moving on* – Engaging again in life. Children often need encouragement to do this.

## Young Children: Toddler to Age 5

It is of paramount importance to conduct pre-planning with regard to how the school will deal with a significant loss. It may be possible to touch on some points of this plan with the students in a gentle, non-threatening way, such as in a Death Education unit. The major goal with young children is to help them realize that no matter what happens, there will always be someone to care for them. The following is a list of suggestions that the school may find helpful in dealing with young children in a crisis situation:

- At the immediate time of the crisis, bring the children together with their family, if possible. Separation from a parent represents a loss of security to children.
- Try to maintain as normal a schedule as possible. Children find security in routines.
- Share feelings with the children. This will encourage the children to share their own feelings. Assure the children that whatever they are feeling (e.g., sadness, anger, confusion) is okay. Provide guidelines of acceptable ways to express feelings. Outlets such as role-play, working with clay or painting may be helpful.
- If the children are very young (i.e., first grade or kindergarten), let them bring a stuffed animal or something familiar with them to school for security.

---

5. Bonnet-Stein, S. (1974) *About dying*. Walker Publishing.

*continued on next page* ▶

- Eliminate any guilt the children may be feeling.
- Clear up misconceptions and answer all questions tactfully, but truthfully.
- Answer the many questions the children will have. It will take time for the children to digest all the facts. If you do not know an answer to a question, do not be afraid to admit it and state that you will try to find out the answer. Do not forget to get back to the student.
- Let the children know that they are cared about. Assure them that they are not facing this situation alone.
- Do not promise anything that cannot be delivered. Psychologists suggest that with a death or divorce it will take a minimum of one year for many children to function normally again, and perhaps as long as five years. Remember that there is no right or wrong way to experience a crisis. The school personnel involved should use their best judgment about what feels best for them and the students in each situation.

## Special Considerations: Ages 6 to 9

In helping children through their loss, the classroom teacher should allow them to be teachers also, especially in relation to experiencing grief. They should be listened to and given the freedom to react differently.

*It is critical that the classroom teacher let go of their own expectations and try to understand those of the child. Listening is more important than guiding and advising.*

Proper words, such as dead, dying and death should be used to eliminate confusion. Using the wrong phrases (e.g., "is asleep," or "went away") will only scare or confuse young children. Questions, no matter how simple, must be answered simply and truthfully, even if the answer is "I don't know." It is important for children to know that there is nothing they could have said or done to make the person die. It is also important to remember that all feelings are normal and that a great service can be provided by just listening and accepting. Most important, the teacher should not be afraid to show emotion. Children need to know that the teacher cares.

The following are points to consider when helping children ages 6 to 9 cope with loss:

- Although children at this age have some understanding of death, the permanence of death is still hard to comprehend.
- Children tend to believe that death is something that happens to others, not themselves.
- Children may believe that the person is alive in the grave.
- Because children may not have the vocabulary to express verbally how they are feeling, they may express it in their behavior.
- Questions may revolve around curiosity about the decomposition of the body and the biological process of death.

## Special Consideration: Ages 9 to 12

Children between ages 9 and 12, have a better understanding of death. Their vocabulary is developed enough to express orally how they feel, but it is unusual if they are able to do so at a time of crisis. Usually their feelings are manifested in their behavior. They may be crying and depressed for a short time, and then out playing shortly after. Although they understand the reality of death better than a young child, they still may believe that death happens to others rather than to themselves. Being understanding is crucial for helping these children handle difficult situations. They need simple, honest and accurate information. As with young children, youth between these ages need reassurance that they are not responsible for the death of loved ones.

Children between ages 9 and 12 are ready for more information such as:

- Why the death happened
- What is a funeral and the reason for funerals
- Will others they love die
- What will happen to them

# Specific Ideas for Elementary Students

The following are ideas that the elementary classroom teacher may use to help when a child is grieving over the loss of a parent, sibling or other significant person in his or her life.

- Let the grieving student be the teacher's helper for the day.
- Provide an opportunity for the child to talk with a respected adult (e.g., their teacher from the previous year, a favorite custodian or cafeteria worker, physical education teacher, counselor, principal).
- Help the child express his or her feelings by working with art materials.
- Facilitate a group hug from the whole class.
- Do not separate or make the child feel apart from the class. At this time, the child needs support from the class.
- Do not single out the grieving student with an open discussion of the personal loss. If the class wants to discuss the loss in the presence of the student, ask for the child's permission to do so.
- Help the child to understand that the feelings surrounding death (i.e., fear, guilt, sadness, anger and shock) are totally normal. Talking about these feelings may help both the child and the class sort them out, which provides an opportunity for personal growth.
- Do not force the child to talk about the death. Most children will do so in their own way and time.
- Encourage classmates to be a support system for both the grieving child and the family. Students at this age will probably need direction from their teacher about how to accomplish this. Sending cards, attending the funeral and taking a collection for flowers are some ways to show support. A discussion of how the class needs to interact with the grieving child upon return to the classroom will be most beneficial.

# Distinguishing Between Normal and Abnormal Grief in Children

At the beginning of the grief process, it is very difficult to distinguish between normal and abnormal grief behavior. Usually, abnormal grief is demonstrated by extreme behavior. The following table includes typical normal and abnormal grief behaviors.

If it has been determined that a child could benefit from counseling, the child should be told so with compassion and understanding. The last thing children need to feel is that something is wrong with them. It may be appropriate to explain to a child that just as there are doctors to help with broken bones, there are caring people who can help in dealing with grief.

| Normal | Abnormal |
|---|---|
| Responds to comfort and support. | Rejects support. |
| Uses play to work out feelings of grief. | Resistant to use of play. |
| Often open and angry. | Complains and is irritable. May not directly express anger. |
| Connects depressed feelings with death. | Does not relate feelings to life events. |
| Can still experience moments of joy. | Projects a pervasive sense of doom. |
| Caring adults can sense a feeling of chronic sadness and emptiness. | Projects hopelessness and emptiness. |
| May express guilt over some aspect of the loss | Has overwhelming feelings of guilt. |
| Self-esteem temporarily impacted. | Deep loss of self-esteem. |

© National Center For Youth Issues • www.ncyi.org • 1-800-477-8277
Please refer to page 2 for duplication information

# Hindrances to Children's Grief

Many factors can delay, distort or hinder the grief process. Therese Rando, an authority on grief in children, identified 14 factors that can make grieving harder for children who have experienced the death of a loved one. The first four factors directly relate to the death of a parental figure.[6]

1. The surviving parent's inability to mourn.
2. The surviving parent's inability to tolerate the pain of the child and allow the child to mourn.
3. Fear about the vulnerability of the surviving parent and the security of self.
4. Ambivalence towards the deceased parent.
5. The lack of security associated with a caring environment.
6. The lack of a caring adult who can stimulate and support the mourning process.
7. Confusion about the death and one's part in it.
8. Unchallenged "magical thinking."
9. An inability to put thoughts, feelings and memories into words.
10. Issues of adolescence that exacerbate normal conflicts in mourning.
11. Cognitive inability to accept the finality and irreversibility of the death.
12. Lack of opportunities to share longing, feelings and memories.
13. Instability of family life after the loss.
14. Reassignment of an inappropriate role and responsibilities.

These factors may contribute to the reason why many children either suppress their grief or have delayed grief reactions. Young people look to adults to show them how to cope with the problems of life. The closest adults in a child's life can have a great impact in helping the child recognize a loss, understand when one is grieving and identify and express feelings in appropriate ways.

## What Adults *Can* Do

The following is a list of basic fundamentals for adults in helping children in the grieving process:

- Get in touch with personal feelings related to the loss. Understand personal skills, knowledge, personal support and information networks.
- Provide opportunities for the expression of the feelings associated with grief. Children who express the pain and feelings of loss are more able to accept that the loss is real and final.
- Listen. Children who are grieving may feel the need to share their feelings over and over. Repeated expression of feelings following a loss is an effective way to get past the initial shock. Listening validates the child and helps build self-esteem. Listening will also help you develop suggestions to help others in commemorating the deceased.
- Provide honest, factual information. Falsehoods feed the fantasies of childhood which can be more terrifying than what really happened.
- Offer assurance and correct any unsound thinking. Address fears and fantasies, correct magical thinking and provide information to normalize grief.
- Encourage and provide for creative expression. Creative expression utilizes the imagination, which is an important mechanism in a child's ability to solve problems.

6. Rondo, T.A. (1992). *How to go on living when someone you love dies.* Bantam Books

- Provide structure and routine to help the child feel safe.

- Offer opportunities for the child to commemorate and remember. It is through these activities that children are able to recognize the meaning of what was lost, and can lean on the strength of the bonds that remain. Remembrance and commemoration also serve as ways that the past can be restored in a new form, so that past experiences can provide learning and become memories for growth.

- Share in a real way. Being a model for children is much more important than being a hero to them. Children need to see that adults hurt too.

- Touch helps. When there are no words, a gentle touch on the shoulder says a lot. Use discretion if you are unsure about touch. A lingering handshake and eye contact may relay a sense of caring and comfort.

## What Adults Should *Not* Do

- Answer children's questions about death with stories and fairy tales.
- Give children unhealthy explanations about death (e.g., "Dad has gone on a long journey").
- Say the deceased "is sleeping now." There is a major difference between sleep and death.
- Push theological beliefs on children.
- Put extra burdens on children, such as the need to care for their family members.

Adults cannot protect children from the reality of death. It has intruded into their lives, and they must face the loss. Adults must help them deal with the loss and hold fast to good memories. Only death makes love possible. Because human life is fragile, it is precious. An individual makes but one appearance on this earth; his or her uniqueness must be cherished.[7] Should a child be protected from discovering that truth?

# Grief in Adolescents

Because of the sorrow of losing a friend, coupled with realizing that they are not immortal, adolescents' inner security systems may become shattered when confronted with the death of a friend or loved one. As part of their coping process, teenagers may exhibit the following:

- Escape by engaging in drugs, sex, etc.
- Decrease of normal inhibitions and increased risk taking.
- Hyper-aggressiveness.
- Defiance.
- Anger at parents or the person who died.
- Suicidal thoughts.
- Fear of close relationships.
- Low self-esteem.
- Guilt.
- Difficulty with long-term plans.
- Short attention span.
- Decline in school work.

7. Leming, M., & Dickerson, G. (1983). *Understanding death, dying, and bereavement.* Holt, Rinehardt and Winston.

These behaviors, if prolonged, may need professional attention. Students need to know, however, that it is normal to feel troubled after experiencing the loss of a loved one. They should be encouraged to find someone to help them through their feelings.

When helping a teenager deal with the death of someone close, it is important for the school staff to understand the following:

- There is little difference in the way teenagers and adults understand death.
- Teenagers need to know that what they are feeling (numbness, sadness, guilt, anger) is normal. Therefore, what they are feeling is okay.
- Teenagers need to know that it is okay to express fear, sadness and love. They need to be free to talk if they so desire.
- Many teenagers act out and verbalize their feelings.
- The teenage years are a time when teens are trying to form their own identity. To accomplish this, they need to have a security system that reassures them that life is basically safe. When they experience a death close to them, their security system is shattered. This makes it more difficult for teenagers to establish their own identity away from their families, making teenage grieving unique when compared to other age groups.
- Dealing with grief is a major undertaking. So is being a teenager.

The following is a list of suggestions for helping a teenager deal with a loss.

- Approach grieving students individually and offer help. Ask for permission before sharing the news of the death in the student's family. Personal information should never be shared if permission is denied. The teacher can ask again later, when appropriate.
- Address the issue carefully. When a student or staff member dies by suicide, issues surrounding the suicide need to be dealt with in the classroom (Refer to Section 2, Crises 2 and 6, for further assistance in dealing with suicide).
- Incorporate a Death Education unit <u>before</u> a death occurs. Many typical teenage attitudes about death (e.g., "it will never happen to me," "I do not have to be concerned about it for 70 years") can be addressed.
- Approach teenagers knowing that they are trying to control their own lives. Many also may feel that they are immortal and that there will be a cure for death by the time they get old.

## Special Consideration: Ages 12 to 18

Although the same philosophy for dealing with grief holds true for students between the ages 12 and 18, frequent classroom changes may cause procedures to vary. In helping children ages 12 to 18 deal with a loss, the following should be considered:

- Older students are usually not as open about their feelings as younger students. They are often embarrassed about expressing their feelings, especially boys.
- It is highly likely that students will not initiate conversations unless they trust you completely. You may need to initiate discussion if you sense the child wants to talk about the deceased. For example you could say, "I know what has happened and I know that this must be very difficult for you. Although you may not agree with me, I think that it is

*continued on next page*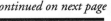

important that we talk about it to make sure you are okay." If the child reacts defensively, an alternative technique is to ask how the student's brother, sister, parent(s), other relatives or friends are handling the death.

- Many adolescents between the ages 12 and 18 feel that they have to be strong and take care of family members who are more open with expressing their grief. As a result, they do not talk about their own grief at home. Therefore, supportive adults at school are extremely important in helping children express their grief. If a student has been talking with another adult outside of school (e.g., minister, counselor), the school worker should regularly inquire if the student is still openly communicating with the adult.

- When a classmate or school staff member dies, it needs to be handled openly at school. Guidelines mentioned in this manual on pages 101-102 should be very useful. When planning activities that relate to talking and sharing about grief, keep in mind that older students may be more accepting of written exercises, rather than verbal.

- Students should be allowed to attend the funeral and decide about a possible memorial.

- In the event of a suicide, watch for signs of suicide contemplation in survivors.

# Suicide Prevention Curriculum

## The Need for Suicide Prevention In Schools

Alarming research shows that the ratio of suicides versus suicide attempts is higher among young people than the elderly. In older populations, approximately 5% to 10% of all attempted suicides result in death. In contrast, the ratio between suicide attempts and deaths among youth is 2 to 1.[11]

According to Edwin Schneidman, a foremost authority on suicide, there may be as many as 250,000 young people attempting suicide each year in the United States and perhaps a million more moving in and out of suicidal crises, thoughts and episodes.[12] The risk that one or more students in a school will attempt or commit suicide is greater today than ever before. Every year parents, teachers and friends are shocked by the suicide of a young person who did not fit their description of a suicidal person. In most cases, something could have been done to save these lives. School teachers and administrators are in a position to recognize potential suicidal students and take action to assist those who cannot, or will not, seek help from family or friends.

---

11. National Center for Injury Prevention and Control.(1992). *Youth suicide prevention programs: A resource guide.* Atlanta, GA: Centers for Disease Control and Prevention
12. Schneidman, E. (1996). *The suicidal mind.* New York: Oxford Press.

# School-Based Suicide Prevention Unit

## Introduction

When instructing a Suicide Prevention Unit, it has been found that using a non-threatening, relaxed approach is more beneficial than one with tightly structured lessons. Teachers need to be sensitive to the feelings and emotions of students in the midst of their peers. The topics of death and suicide can, at times, be overwhelming to students. Therefore, when students are called upon, they need to be able to choose not to talk without penalty. Teachers must also be flexible in relation to the time allocated to classroom discussion. Some discussions may take longer than originally planned, and adjustments may have to be made in lesson plans or the number of class periods needed.

For teachers, respect, sensitivity, flexibility and compassion are essential in their approach. Asking students ahead of time what topics they feel ought to be included in the unit will convey the message that the subjects (suicide and death) will be approached in an honest and meaningful way. An important component of a Suicide Prevention Unit is a discussion of the reality of death, what it is, what it means and students' attitudes toward it.

Teaching methods should include classroom discussions, *short* lectures to present facts, stories and role playing activities. In addition, innovative methods of evaluation, such as skits, can be effective replacements for more traditional methods (i.e., written tests). It is important that teaching methods address the music that is popular with students, as some lyrics contain messages and attitudes about suicide.

It is the intent of a school-based Suicide Prevention Unit to:

1. Stress to youth that suicide is an unacceptable and tragic, irreversible act.
2. Help educators and students recognize and get assistance for potential suicidal youth.
3. Help educators and students get in touch with both their feelings on death and the reality of death.

## Unit Objectives

1. Educators will uncover attitudes about suicide that are prevalent among their students.
2. Educators and students will dispel the social norm that suicide is something not to be discussed.
3. Educators and students will replace misconceptions and misinformation about suicide with facts.
4. Educators and students will be able to recognize when someone is suicidal and know how to get help for that person.
5. Educators and students will realize that a completed suicide is irreversible. They will understand that suicide is a permanent solution to a temporary problem.

# Interdisciplinary Middle School Suicide Prevention Unit

One approach for teaching suicide prevention in middle school is coordinating concepts in an interdisciplinary unit. This team approach allows teachers from different subject areas to work together and coordinate lessons. Teaming is an integral part of the middle school concept and by utilizing all available resources, including human resources, the concept of the Suicide Prevention Unit will be easier to grasp and more meaningful for students. The following is an example of an interdisciplinary Suicide Prevention Unit. It provides general ideas, allows for creativity by the classroom teachers and can be expanded or modified to fit the needs of a particular group of students.

## Sample Unit

Students in the sixth through eighth grades meet with their teachers in a large meeting room (e.g., library, multipurpose room) to introduce the Suicide Prevention Unit and the reasons for including it in the educational program. During this meeting, teachers present the theme of the unit and explain why the particular theme was selected. In addition, slogans for the unit can be elicited from, discussed among and voted on by the students. It is suggested that no more than three slogans be adopted to prevent losing focus of the main purpose of the unit.

The number of class periods needed to cover the unit may vary from course to course depending on the depth of material. For example, Math may only need two or three class periods while English and Social Studies may need an entire week. This is acceptable as long as closure for the entire unit follows the same format as the introductory meeting. The purpose of the closure meeting is to summarize the main concepts of the unit, review the theme and slogans and obtain student feedback.

The following is an example of incorporating suicide prevention concepts into core curricular learning objectives.

## Math

> *Objective:* Students will do a series of raw data calculation exercises to identify the scope of the current teenage suicide epidemic.

### *Activities:*

1. Figure the percentage of increase over the last 10 years for age groups: 15 to 24, 25 to 39, 40 to 55, 56 and over.
2. Make graphs and charts showing the results of activity 1.
3. Figure the percentage of suicide attempts to suicide deaths for age groups: 15 to 24, 25 to 39, 40 to 55, 56 and over.
4. Make graphs and charts showing the results of activity 3.
5. Make a pie graph showing the percentages of methods used by males ages 15 to 24, who have attempted suicide.
6. Make a pie graph showing the percentages of methods used by females ages 15 to 24, who have attempted suicide.
7. Write a two-page paper summarizing observations of the data calculated in activities 1-6.
8. If access to a computer-lab is available, have the students report their findings and statistics.

© National Center For Youth Issues • www.ncyi.org • 1-800-477-8277
Please refer to page 2 for duplication information

## Science

*Objective*: Students will learn to understand and identify the causes and consequences of suicide.

*Activities*:

1. Discuss physiology and definition of death.
2. Discuss the effects of knives, bullets, poison and fire on the human body.
3. Discuss stress and its effects on the body and mind.
4. If resources are available, invite a guest who can further stress the impact and effects of the above.

## English

*Objective*: Students will become familiar with attitudes toward suicide and the problems it causes as presented in literature and music.

*Activities*:

1. Read *Remembering The Good Times*, by Richard Peck.
   a. Why does one of the main characters commit suicide?
   b. What leads him to suicide, and what could have prevented him from committing suicide?
2. Read William Shakespeare's *Romeo and Juliet*.
   a. What is Shakespeare's attitude about taking one's own life?
3. Explore contemporary music for attitudes and messages conveyed (e.g., Kurt Cobain and Nirvana).

## Social Studies

*Objective*: Students will learn (1) to recognize the signs of a potential suicide victim, and (2) some practical methods to help suicidal individuals get proper assistance.

*Activities*:

1. Discuss the sheet **"How to Recognize a Potentially Suicidal Person"** (see page 151).
2. Discuss how to help a potentially suicidal person.
3. Develop and role-play vignettes demonstrating skills learned in activities 1 and 2.
4. Discuss community agencies that can help suicidal individuals.
5. Investigate grief and effects of suicide on friends and family:
   a. What do the friends and family go through?
   b. How does society judge them?
   c. How do they deal with guilt?
6. Produce an infomercial that includes their findings and lists help agencies.

**NOTE:** Teachers are encouraged to make modifications to the above sample interdisciplinary unit to fit the particular needs of their students. Instead of four written evaluations, it is suggested that teachers develop one interdisciplinary test or have students perform skits as a means of evaluation.

# High School Suicide Prevention Unit

Inserting activities pertaining to suicide prevention into existing courses can be beneficial. The following are examples of how suicide topics can be integrated into existing courses.

- English – A discussion of plays that either dramatize or glamorize suicide can present an opportunity to explore the realities of suicide.
- Science – Discussion of the physiology of death.
- Psychology – The psychological state of a suicidal individual and how a person arrived at this frame of mind.
- Social Studies – Discussion of laws dealing with suicide, active and passive euthanasia, and the social consequences of suicide. In addition, lessons pertaining to developing friendships and getting along with others.
- Health Education – The concepts of suicide prevention can easily fit into the framework of a Health Education course. The following section consists of a sample unit on suicide prevention for the high school Health Education teacher. This unit is only a framework, thus leaving the fine details and teaching methods up to the individual classroom teacher.

## Sample Unit For Health Education Course

### Section One

#### Objectives:

1. Help students understand the meaning of death.
2. Identify students' feelings about their own death and how to deal with their feelings.
3. Help students understand that, by talking about death, we can learn to appreciate life and live in a more loving and fulfilling manner.
4. Explore students' thoughts about suicide and the views others have about suicide.

#### Activities:

1. Definition of death exercise – Divide students into groups and have them write down as many synonyms for the word death as they can identify. After five minutes, have the groups share their list of synonyms while the teacher writes the terms on the chalk board. When the groups are done sharing, review the terms on the board stressing their finality and irreversibility, and stress that everyone, at some point, experiences this fate. (Activity relates to Objectives 1, 2 and 3)

2. Students' goals and dreams – Divide students into groups and have them discuss experiences they are most looking forward to in life. Then have groups discuss if they were to die today, which goals and dreams in life would not be reached. (Activity relates to Objective 3)

3. Questionnaire on death – Have students individually complete the questionnaire "**Getting in Touch With My Feelings About Death**" (see page 145). Explain that the obituary is to get them to identify what is really important in their lives and also to motivate them to reach the goals and dreams they have set for themselves. After completion of the questionnaire, break the class down into groups of two or three to quietly share their answers with each other. (Activity relates to objectives 1, 2 and 3)

4. Class discussion on suicide – As a result of student discussions on the topic of death, the class should be more at ease with a discussion of suicide. This will free students to examine their own feelings and the feelings of others. The following questions will help guide a discussion about suicide. (Activity relates to Objective 4):

    a. Have you ever known someone who committed or attempted suicide? (No names need to be given)

    b. If so, what was your reaction?

    c. How did you feel and what were your thoughts?

    d. How did other people react?

## Section Two

Suicide is not confined to any social, economic, racial or religious groups. It is prevalent in all socioeconomic settings. Many times, the students who commit suicide are individuals whom others would least expect to do so. Often, these students are quiet, easily overlooked and relatively well behaved.

### Objectives:

1. Realize that anyone can become suicidal.
2. Separate fact from myth about teenage suicide. Refer to **"Common Myths About Teen Suicide"** page. (see page 147)

### Activities:

1. **"Quiet Cries"** – Students either read or act out the roles in the play **"Quiet Cries."**[13] After the play, students identify and discuss the signs and clues emitted by the characters. (Activity relates to Objectives 1 and 2)

2. Class discussion and/or writing assignment – Students divide into groups and are assigned one of the following statements:

   • The straight A student is never a potentially suicidal person.

   • The student whose parents are highly successful business people is rarely a candidate for suicide.

   • The student with older siblings who have experienced academic and athletic successes is usually not a person who becomes suicidal.

   • The only students at risk for suicide are those who come from broken homes and struggle with their schoolwork.

Students are asked to either agree or disagree with the statements and list the reasons why. The teacher then passes out **"Common Myths About Teen Suicide"** for discussion (see page 147). (Activity relates to Objectives 1 and 2)

---

13. Blake, E. (1970). *Quiet cries; A play about suicide prevention suitable for presentation by amateur drama groups.* Chevy Chase, Md: National Institute of Mental Health; for sale by the Supt. of Docs., U.S. Govt. Print. Off., Washington.

## Section Three

Most people who commit suicide have been thinking about it for some time before the act. They often exhibit subtle clues.

### Objectives:

1. Recognize possible warning signs of suicide.
2. Examine and discuss possible causes of suicide.
3. Examine assessment methods to determine the seriousness of a suicidal individual.

### Activities:

1. Short lecture and discussion on the recognition of warning signs – Hand out "**Suicide Warning Signs**" (see page 136 ), and ask for comments on each of the 10 items on the list. Students identify whether any of these warning signs were exhibited in someone they have known who attempted or committed suicide. (Activity relates to Objectives 1 and 2)

2. Suicide causes – Divide the class into four groups with each group being assigned two of the eight causes of suicide (see "**Suicide Causes**", page 150). The group writes reasons why these situations cause people to think about taking their lives. Each group then shares their reasons with the class. Encourage discussion after each group finishes. (Activity relates to Objective 2)

3. Suicide assessment using the SLAP Method – Make a transparency from the "**Suicide Assessment-SLAP Method**" printout (see page 149) to use on an overhead projector. Explain the SLAP Method to the class, ask questions and encourage discussion. Encourage students to share related experiences. (Activity relates to Objective 3)

## Section Four

Once students have learned to recognize a potentially suicidal person, they need to know what to do to get help for the person.

### Objectives:

1. Help students realize that talking to suicidal persons about their feelings, rather than ignoring them, can help.
2. Help students realize that telling a responsible person that someone has shown signs of being suicidal is extremely important.
3. Identify sources within the community that can help in suicide prevention.

### Activities:

1. Classroom discussion on "How We Can Help" – Hand out "**Suicide: How We Can Help**" (see page 152). Have class discuss the 11 items on this list and encourage their input during the discussion. For number 8 on the hand out, have students make a list of people and other community agencies that can be of help. (Activity relates to Objectives 2 and 3)

© National Center For Youth Issues • www.ncyi.org • 1-800-477-8277
Please refer to page 2 for duplication information

2. Class discussion on when it is time to break confidentiality – Divide class into equal groups and have them discuss the following questions:

- If your friend told you he (she) was seriously considering suicide and asked you to not tell anybody, would you?
- If you would tell, when and whom would you tell?
- Under what conditions would you go to a teacher, responsible adult or community agency, rather than to your friend's parents?

Give students at least 20 minutes to discuss these questions, with one person writing down responses. Have a spokesperson from each group share the answers with the class. (Activity relates to Objective 2.)

> **NOTE:** The teacher needs to stress that if a friend requests confidentiality, students should try to respect his/her need for secrecy. Concern for confidentiality, however, is a secondary concern compared to their friend's life.)

3. Identify sources of professional help in the community – Divide the class into three groups. Assign each group one of the following:
- Identify and make a list of local suicide prevention services.
- List the crisis intervention services offered by local hospitals.
   List the crisis intervention services offered by county mental health agencies.

Collect the information from each group and make a directory of services for distribution to all students. (Activity relates to Objective 3)

## Evaluation Plan

The following evaluation plan can serve as a guide for the classroom teacher in determining the effect the Suicide Prevention Unit had on students. Three plans are presented; the first two are written exams and the third is a collection of vignettes the students can role play for the class or school that demonstrates skills in recognizing suicidal clues and helping suicidal individuals.

*Written Test One* – Pre- and Post-test.

Students write their ideas and thoughts about death and suicide on the first day of the Suicide Prevention Unit (Pre-test). At the completion of the unit, the students are handed their Pre-test and must write a statement about how their attitudes have been changed or reinforced.

*Written Test Two* – Essay test.

   *Directions* – Answer the following questions in written detail.

1. You feel that one of your friends is suicidal and may soon hurt him/herself.
   a. Would it be proper to go behind your friend's back and approach an adult who could help? Why or why not?

b. How might your suicidal friend react toward you when he/she finds out you betrayed their trust?

c. How would you feel if the suicidal friend committed suicide and even though you knew he or she might, you did not seek help because you did not want to betray a trust?

2. Why do experts say suicide knows no racial, economic, social or intellectual barriers?

3. Make a list of school and community resource people who can help a suicidal friend who you feel is in immediate danger.

*Test Three* – Role Plays.

The following four examples are for student skits that can be used as a means of evaluation. Students perform these skits, demonstrating recognition and helping skills learned from the instructional part of the Suicide Prevention Unit. These skits may be performed in front of the class, for the entire school or for the community.

1. Your cousin is very heavy into cocaine. She has been stealing to support her drug use and is obviously addicted. She realizes her addiction and does not want to steal anymore to support her habit. She calls you on the telephone and tells you that she realizes she has hurt the people she loves, yet she feels she cannot live without the drug. She says the only alternative is to kill herself. You feel she is close to committing suicide. How could you respond to her on the phone to convince her not to do it?

3. Joshua is our close friend who wants to be perfect in everything he does. He is an honor student, and when he does not get an A on a test, he cries. The other day in gym class he cried when his volleyball team lost a game. Yesterday, he became extremely nervous and got the "shakes" before a math test. You get the feeling that Joshua's self-inflicted pressure is causing frustration. You become worried that this behavior may be suicidal. What would you do to help Joshua?

4. Elizabeth is an 18 year-old high school senior who considers herself a social outcast. She is an average student who does not seem (by her own admission) to excel in anything. She is very depressed because the senior prom is quickly approaching, and no boy has ever asked her out on a date or shown any interest in her. She is very depressed and sees no hope for an acceptable social life or ever getting married. She begins to talk about taking her life. You are one of her few close friends. How could you help her? What could you do and say?

5. A friend of yours was recently arrested for drug possession. Although he is not a regular user, he feels devastated that he has hurt his parents. He feels extremely humiliated because, in his eyes, he has caused great embarrassment to his entire family. He has become despondent. You get the feeling that he may be considering ending it all permanently. You really want to help. What could and what would you do?

---

**NOTE**: The exercise pages mentioned in this section may be found in Section 5 of this manual. **"Getting In Touch With my Feelings About Death"** (see page 145), **"Common Myths About Teen Suicide"** (see page 147), **"Suicide Assessment-SLAP Method"** (see page 149), **"Suicide Causes"** (see page 150), **"Suicide: How We Can Help"** (see page 152).

# References

1. National Center for Health Statistics. (1997). Atlanta, GA: Centers for Disease Control and Prevention.

2. Wolheht, A. (1996). *Healing and the bereaved child.* Compassion Press.

3. Grollman, E. (1974). *Death: A practical guide for living.* Beacon Press.

4. Mothers Against Drunk Driving. (1992). Guidelines and suggestions when handling a loss. Newsletter, 2-3.

5. Bonnet-Stein, S. (1974). *About dying.* Walker Publishing.

6. Rondo, T. A. (1992). *How to go on living when someone you love dies.* Bantam Books.

7. Leming, M., & Dickerson, G. (1983). *Understanding death, dying, and bereavement.* Holt, Rinehardt and Winston.

8. Michigan Association of Suicidology. (1997).

9. Gordon, S. (1989). *When living hurts.*

10. Klagsbrun, F. (1984). *Too young to die.*

11. National Center for Injury Prevention and Control. (1992). *Youth suicide prevention programs: A resource guide.* Atlanta, GA: Centers for Disease Control and Prevention.

12. Schneidman, E. (1996). *The suicidal mind.* New York: Oxford Press.

13. Blake, E. (1970). *Quiet cries; A play about suicide prevention suitable for presentation by amateur drama groups.* Chevy Chase, Md: National Institute of Mental Health; for sale by the Supt. of Docs., U.S. Govt. Print. Off., Washington.

# Section 5

# Crisis Response
# Planning Worksheets

This section contains 20 worksheets presented and utilized throughout this manual. You will find a list of each section's specific worksheets at the end of each section.

> **NOTE:** The authors and publisher give permission to the owner of this manual to copy the contents of this section as needed for educational and crisis management purposes. These pages are not to be used for resale.

# Community Resources Sheet

## Names and Phone Numbers of Outside Resources

**Psychologist:** _____    ( ___ ) _____

_____    ( ___ ) _____

**Social Workers:** _____    ( ___ ) _____

_____    ( ___ ) _____

**Funeral Directors:** _____    ( ___ ) _____

_____    ( ___ ) _____

**Clergy:** _____    ( ___ ) _____

_____    ( ___ ) _____

**Others:** _____    ( ___ ) _____

_____    ( ___ ) _____

# Crisis Response Checklist

Date: _____    Crisis: _____

Person responsible for checklist: _____

☐ 1. Notify police (if appropriate).

☐ 2. Notify the superintendent and assistant superintendent(s).

☐ 3. Assemble the Crisis Response Team. Develop a specific plan and assign roles to members of the team.

☐ 4. Notify the individual's family of the school's plan.

☐ 5. Use a phone tree to notify staff of the crisis and inform them that all media inquiries are to be directed to _____. Set a time for an emergency staff meeting.

☐ 6. At the staff meeting, provide written communication to all staff as to when and how students will be informed of the tragedy, guidelines for class discussions, plans for the day, etc.

☐ 7. Set a time to inform all students and give staff a prepared statement.

☐ 8. Provide students and staff with opportunities to discuss their feelings and concerns.

☐ 9. Set aside Crisis Rooms for students and staff.
Student Crisis Room staffed by: _____.
Staff Crisis Room staffed by: _____.

☐ 10. Inform administrators at other schools that siblings, relatives and friends attend to watch for special needs of grieving students.

☐ 11. Inform significant other adults on a need-to-know basis.

☐ 12. Enlist the help of staff members to identify students who may be struggling with the grieving process.

© National Center For Youth Issues • www.ncyi.org • 1-800-477-8277
Please refer to page 2 for duplication information

# School Faculty and Staff Issues

## Develop a notification chain

1. How will the information be passed along to all faculty members?

_____

_____

_____

2. Who will gather the facts?

_____

_____

## Roles of the faculty/staff

1. Who is responsible for what?

_____

_____

_____

_____

2. Who will substitute for faculty/staff absence or unavailability?

_____

_____

_____

## Secretary/Receptionist

1. Are secretaries/receptionists prepared to handle incoming calls regarding the crisis?

☐ Yes    ☐ No

2. How will they respond to requests for information?

_____

_____

## Crisis Response Team

1. Are team members available?  ☐ Yes  ☐ No
2. What are the guidelines for each position?

_____

_____

_____

_____

_____

3. Where will the team set up (physical space)?

_____

_____

_____

_____

4. Have appropriate outside community agencies been contacted?

_____

_____

_____

_____

5. Are the agencies in agreement with the school's plan?

_____

_____

_____

## Informing students

1. How will the students learn of the crisis facts?

_____

_____

_____

2. Has a prepared statement been written? ☐ Yes ☐ No

3. When will they be informed? _____

## Community Issues

### Parents

1. Have parents been notified of the crisis, school policy and response actions taken?
☐ Yes ☐ No

2. Whom can parents contact with questions or concerns?

_____

_____

_____

_____

_____

_____

1. What information may and may not be released?
2. What access will the media have to the family, staff, students and school grounds?

_____

_____

_____

_____

_____

3. Have contacts been established to ensure boundaries, intentions and understandings of policy and procedures? ☐ Yes      ☐ No

# Evaluation Issues

## Information Logging/Recording

1. Are the forms or guidelines in place to keep a complete history of the events, phone calls, released information, etc.?   ☐ Yes    ☐ No

## Concerns Related to Tragedy Response Planning and Policy

1. Does every member of the school community have access to or own a copy of the policy?
   ☐ Yes      ☐ No

2. Does the policy include a roster of names and assigned roles relating to the crises plan?
   ☐ Yes      ☐ No

3. How often will this plan be reviewed?

_____

_____

_____

# Tragedy Response Implementation Plan

## I.   Team Members

| Name | Phone Number | e-mail |
|------|--------------|--------|
|      |              |        |
|      |              |        |
|      |              |        |
|      |              |        |
|      |              |        |
|      |              |        |
|      |              |        |
|      |              |        |
|      |              |        |
|      |              |        |
|      |              |        |
|      |              |        |
|      |              |        |
|      |              |        |
|      |              |        |
|      |              |        |

## II.   Team Roles and Responsibilities

### A. *Team Leader*

Name: _____ Phone #: _____

Responsibility: _____

_____

_____

_____

_____

_____

_____

_____

_____

_____

_____

## B. Family Liaison

Name: _____ Phone #: _____

Responsibility: _____

_____

_____

_____

_____

## C. Media Liaison

Name: _____ Phone #: _____

Responsibility: _____

_____

_____

_____

_____

## D. Roamers

Name: _____ Phone #: _____

Name: _____ Phone #: _____

Name: _____ Phone #: _____

Name: _____ Phone #: _____

Responsibility: _____

_____

_____

_____

_____

## E. Counselors

Name: _____ Phone #: _____

Name: _____ Phone #: _____

Name: _____ Phone #: _____

Name: _____ Phone #: _____

Responsibility: _____

_____

_____

_____

### F. Other

Social Worker: _____ Phone #: _____

Social Worker:_____ Phone #: _____

Social Worker: _____ Phone #: _____

Social Worker:_____ Phone #: _____

School Psychologist: _____ Phone #: _____

School Psychologist:_____ Phone #: _____

## III. Notification Chain

A. *Name:* _____ *Phone #:* _____

Responsibility: Will notify bus drivers. Must have phone list and may need to develop a sub-chain if the list is long.

B. *Name:* _____ *Phone #:* _____

Responsibility: Will activate chain to notify teachers. Must have a copy of the teacher phone chain.

C. *Name:* _____ *Phone #:* _____

*Responsibility:* Will activate chain to notify support staff (e.g., aides, custodians, secretaries). Must have a copy of the support staff phone chain.

D. *Name:* _____ *Phone #:* _____

*Responsibility:* Will notify superintendent, school board and other building administrators.

## IV. Community Resources

A. Local Pastor: _____ Phone #: _____

B. Local Police/Sheriff_____ Phone #: _____

C. State Police _____ Phone #: _____

D. Emergency Medical Services _____ Phone #: _____

E. Fire Department Rescue Team _____ Phone #: _____

F. Hospital: _____ Phone #: _____

G. Poison Control Center _____ Phone #: _____

H. Community Mental Health _____ Phone #: _____

I. Department of Social Services _____ Phone #: _____

J. Crisis Intervention Hot Line: _____ Phone #: _____

## V. Informing the School Family

A. How will students be informed? _____

_____
_____
_____
_____
_____
_____
_____

B. Prepared statement for classroom teachers? (Use specific statements identified in Section 2.)

_____
_____
_____
_____
_____
_____
_____
_____
_____
_____
_____
_____
_____
_____
_____
_____
_____
_____
_____
_____
_____
_____
_____

## VI. Crisis Rooms

### *A. Student Crisis Room*

Staffed By: _____   Room # _____

### *B. Staff Crisis Room*

Staffed By: _____   Room #: _____

## VII. Informing Parents

A. How will parents be notified of the crisis? _____

_____

_____

_____

_____

_____

_____

B. Whom can parents contact with questions and concerns?

Name: _____   Phone #: _____

Name: _____   Phone #: _____

## VIII. Information Logging

A. The Crisis Response Team Leader (or _____) will keep a complete history of events, phone calls and released information.

B. Report of incident and school's response will be recorded and filed by:

_____

_____

C. Location where the file of the incident is stored: _____

_____

_____

## IX.  Post Crisis

A. The next time a crisis occurs, we want the following changes to take place:

_____

_____

_____

_____

_____

_____

B. To prepare for future crises, we need to add:

_____

_____

_____

_____

_____

_____

_____

C. To prepare for future crises, we need to delete:

_____

_____

_____

_____

_____

_____

_____

_____

# Student Funeral Home Visitation Form

After the tragic death of a classmate or staff member at school, many students may wish to or are encouraged to go to the funeral home visitation, funeral, or wake service. The crisis team needs to take into consideration that students will need comfort and support at these functions and have an organized system of staff volunteers ready to serve.

> **NOTE:** Some cultures and religions may be very unfamiliar to students. The crisis team should prepare students for the unfamiliar customs and practices of these cultures and/or religions and instruct about appropriate behavior at these functions.

The following is a sample form for a funeral home visitation:

---

## Funeral Home Visitation Sign-up

Name of Funeral Home: _____

Date: _____          Date: _____

Time: ___:___ AM/PM - ___:___ AM/PM          Time: ___:___ AM/PM - ___:___ AM/PM

| Date | Time | Staff Members |
|------|------|---------------|
| _____ | ___:___ AM/PM to ___:___ AM/PM | _____ _____ |
| _____ | ___:___ AM/PM to ___:___ AM/PM | _____ _____ |
| _____ | ___:___ AM/PM to ___:___ AM/PM | _____ _____ |
| _____ | ___:___ AM/PM to ___:___ AM/PM | _____ _____ |
| _____ | ___:___ AM/PM to ___:___ AM/PM | _____ _____ |
| _____ | ___:___ AM/PM to ___:___ AM/PM | _____ _____ |
| _____ | ___:___ AM/PM to ___:___ AM/PM | _____ _____ |
| _____ | ___:___ AM/PM to ___:___ AM/PM | _____ _____ |
| _____ | ___:___ AM/PM to ___:___ AM/PM | _____ _____ |
| _____ | ___:___ AM/PM to ___:___ AM/PM | _____ _____ |
| _____ | ___:___ AM/PM to ___:___ AM/PM | _____ _____ |
| _____ | ___:___ AM/PM to ___:___ AM/PM | _____ _____ |
| _____ | ___:___ AM/PM to ___:___ AM/PM | _____ _____ |
| _____ | ___:___ AM/PM to ___:___ AM/PM | _____ _____ |
| _____ | ___:___ AM/PM to ___:___ AM/PM | _____ _____ |
| _____ | ___:___ AM/PM to ___:___ AM/PM | _____ _____ |

---

# Student Personal Resource Survey

Name: _____

Friends on whom I can count: _____
_____
_____
_____
_____

Family members with whom I feel comfortable sharing my feelings: _____
_____
_____
_____

Relative (e.g., aunt, uncle, cousin, grandparent) with whom I can talk: _____
_____
_____
_____
_____

Faculty and staff (e.g., teacher, counselor, coach) I can go to for support:
_____
_____
_____
_____

Someone I might be able to count on even though we are not always close:
_____
_____
_____
_____
_____

# Suicidal Behavior Reporting Form

Date: _____

Student's Name: _____ Grade: _____

Telephone: _____ Birth Date: _____

Person Submitting Report: _____

School: _____

Address: _____

City: _____ State: _____

How did you become aware of the student's suicidal threat/action? _____

_____

_____

_____

Describe the incident and/or situation surrounding threat/action (e.g., personal difficulties, school problems). _____

_____

_____

_____

What was the means used or threatened (e.g., weapon, instrument, drug)? _____

_____

Lethality: Low ☐    Medium ☐    High ☐

Designated staff person responsible for contacting parents. _____

Which family member was contacted? _____

_____

Parent Contacted: Yes ☐    No ☐

Parental Response: _____

_____

_____

_____

_____

## Follow Up

Date: _____ Who: _____

Action: _____

_____

_____

_____

# Suicide Warning Signs

Behavioral clues that a suicidal person might exhibit include the following;

1. Previous threats or attempts at suicide.

2. Support for an important role model who committed suicide.

3. Feelings of being a failure.

4. Radical personality changes (e.g., persistent sadness, loss of interest in usual activities).

5. Withdrawal from family, friends and regular activities.

6. Noticeable changes in eating or sleeping habits.

7. Neglect in personal appearance.

8. A decline in the quality of school work.

9. Violent or rebellious behavior.

10. Drug or alcohol abuse.

11. Verbal hints (e.g., "I will not be a problem for you much longer," or "Nothing matters").

12. Giving away favorite possessions.

13. Suddenly becoming cheerful after a prolonged depression (which may indicate the decision to commit suicide has been made).

*If students or staff display some or all of the above behaviors, the following questions will help in further identifying the seriousness of the risk.*

- Has that person had a recent major loss of a loved one?

- Has there been a recent major disappointment or humiliation in this person's life?

- Has there been a sudden lack of communication between this person and teachers, friends or family?

- Is there evidence of an unstable home life?

- Does this person exhibit feelings of revenge against a former love interest, parent or another person?

Consider suicidal acts, however lethal, as being an effort to stop unbearable anguish or intolerable pain. Often, suicide can be prevented by letting others know about a person's struggles, breaking what could be a fatal secret, offering help, getting loved ones interested and responsive, creating action around the person at risk and showing the individual that someone loves and cares about them. It short, it is better to do something than nothing.

© National Center For Youth Issues • www.ncyi.org • 1-800-477-8277
Please refer to page 2 for duplication information

# Parental Agreement/Release Form

Having met with member(s) of the Crisis Response Team and having discussed concerns about my
child _____
(child's name- please print)

regarding _____

I, _____
(parents name- please print)

☐   Agree to cooperate and follow through with the recommendations made.

☐   Disagree with the recommendations made and take full responsibility for the welfare of
my child and any outcome of this crisis.

☐   Understand that the welfare of children is a shared responsibility and that if no help
is sought for a child at risk that state and federal laws require notification of Child
Protective Services for further investigation.

Parents/Guardians signature _____

Principal signature _____

Crisis Response Team Representative signature _____

Follow Up _____

_____

Date: _____

Who: _____

Action: _____

_____

_____

_____

cc: Principal's Confidential File/Superintendent

# Student/Teacher Worksheet For Homicide Assembly

***Directions:*** Use this worksheet as a discussion outline to educate students about personal safety and how to make the school safer. Do not give to students to simply fill in answers. Rather, use as a point for class discussion.

1. List the possible ways students can live a safer life: _____

_____

_____

_____

_____

_____

_____

_____

_____

_____

_____

_____

_____

2. List the two main ways homicide occurs:

   a. _____

_____

   b. _____

_____

3. Discuss ways the school could be made safer:

_____

_____

_____

_____

_____

_____

_____

_____

_____

_____

# Student/Teacher Worksheet For First HIV Assembly

***Directions:*** To encourage discussion of this subject, this worksheet is to be completed as a verbal exercise by the entire class. It should ***not*** be handed out to students for them to fill in on their own.

1. List the possible ways of transmitting HIV:

    a)_____

    b)_____

    c) _____

    d) _____

    e) _____

    f) _____

2. List the two main ways the HIV virus is spread:

    a) _____

    b) _____

3. HIV/AIDS is *not* spread by casual contact. Define casual contact.

    _____

    _____

    _____

    _____

    _____

4. If we do not engage in the two behaviors listed in item #2, would a student with HIV be a danger to the rest of the student body? Why or why not?

    _____

    _____

    _____

    _____

    _____

    _____

    _____

    _____

# Student/Teacher Worksheet For Second HIV Assembly

***Directions:*** To encourage discussion of this subject, this worksheet is to be completed as a verbal exercise by the entire class. (***Note:*** Teachers may wish to make a transparency and put it on an overhead projector instead of handing this out in worksheet form.)

1. It was very difficult for Ryan White and his family to deal with the fact that he had AIDS. How did the community add to this difficulty?

_____

_____

_____

_____

_____

2. Why do you think the people who lived in the community reacted to Ryan and his family the way they did?

_____

_____

_____

_____

_____

3. Why did students and people in Cicero, Indiana, treat Ryan White differently than in the community in which he grew up?

_____

_____

_____

_____

4. As members of the school community, how should we treat those who are HIV positive?

_____

_____

_____

_____

_____

# HIV Crisis Classroom Discussion

**Directions:** The teacher is to read the following story to the class and then *discuss* the questions that follow. (**Note:** A transparency of this story on an overhead projector may be very helpful for students to refer to during the discussion.)

"William has AIDS. He has Kaposi's Sarcoma, and some of the purplish blotches from the disease have started to show on his face. He has come to a public swimming pool and paid the admission fee. As people are lined up after their shower to enter the pool, the lifeguard recognizes the blotches on William's face as a sign of AIDS. As a result, the lifeguard refuses to let William into the pool area. William refuses to get out of line and prevents others from getting into the pool area. You are behind William in line and want to go swimming. You become increasingly impatient. Some people in line start yelling at the lifeguard. Others yell at William."

1. If you were in line behind William, what would you do?

   _____

   _____

   _____

2. What do you think would have been the best thing for William to do in this situation?

   _____

   _____

   _____

3. What should the lifeguard have done in this situation?

   _____

   _____

   _____

   _____

4. Should people with HIV/AIDS be allowed to swim in public swimming pools?

   _____

   Why or why not? _____

   _____

5. If you were the pool recreation director, what kind of policy do you think you might set for situations like this?

   _____

   _____

   _____

   _____

# Getting In Touch With My Feelings About Death

When _____ died,

(name of loved one)

I felt: _____

_____

_____

If I could do three things before I die, they would be:

1._____

_____

_____

2._____

_____

_____

3._____

_____

_____

My greatest fear about death is: _____

_____

_____

_____

My greatest comfort when thinking about death is: _____

_____

_____

_____

By faith, I believe that death: _____

_____

_____

_____

In view of death, what would I change in my life?_____

_____

_____

_____

Under what circumstances would I find death acceptable?_____
_____
_____

I think my own death will be: _____
_____
_____
_____

After death there is: _____
_____
_____
_____

---

**My Obituary:**

_____, age _____, died yesterday as a

result of _____.

He/she was a member of _____.

He/she is survived by _____.

He/she will be missed by _____

because _____. People will notice the loss of

his/her contribution in _____. He/she always

wanted, but never had the opportunity to _____

_____.

Charitable donations may be sent to _____.

---

# Common Myths About Teen Suicide[3,9,10]

*Myth*: Youth who talk about suicide rarely attempt it.
**Fact**:  Most who attempt or commit suicide have given verbal clues.

*Myth*: Talking about suicide will make it happen.
**Fact**:  Talking about suicide does not place ideas into young people's heads that are not already there. There is evidence that once a suicide occurs, others may follow as a contagious reaction to hopelessness.

*Myth*: The tendency towards suicide is inherited.
**Fact**:  There is no evidence of a genetic link. A previous suicide in the family, however, may establish a destructive model for dealing with stress and depression.

*Myth*: Teenage suicides happen at night.
**Fact**:  Most teenage suicides occur between 3:00 and 6:00 in the afternoon, presumably when the suicidal person can be seen and stopped.

*Myth*: Suicidal people leave notes.
**Fact**:  Only a small number, approximately 15%, leave notes.

*Myth*: If a person wants to commit suicide, nothing can stop them.
**Fact**:  Suicidal people have mixed feelings about death. They often send out messages and clues that point to their pain. No one is suicidal all the time. Many suicides can be prevented.

*Myth*: Youth who want to commit suicide are mentally ill.
**Fact**:  Mental illness increases the risk of suicide. Most young people who attempt or commit suicide, however, would not be diagnosed as mentally ill. Youth suicide is often a sudden and urgent reaction to accumulative events and stress.

*Myth:* A teenager who has been suicidal is never out of danger.
**Fact:**  Many youth who have been depressed recover and lead normal, healthy lives. They learn constructive, rather than destructive, ways to cope with feelings and disappointments.

3.   Grollman, E. (1974). *Death: A practical guide for living. Beacon Press.*
9.   Gordon, S. (1989). *When living hurts.*
10.  Klagsbrun, F. (1984). *Too young to die.*

# Suicide Facts

The following suicide facts are based on official statistics published by the American Association of Suicidology.[8]

1. Currently, there are slightly more than 30,000 suicides annually. That is 83 suicides per day or one suicide every 17 minutes.

2. Rates of suicide are highest in the western regions, especially the mountain states.

3. Suicide is the eighth leading cause of death in the U.S.

4. Males commit suicide at rates three to four times that of females.

5. Firearms are the most often used method for suicide.

6. Suicide rates have traditionally decreased in times of wars and increased in times of economic crises.

7. Spring and Mondays consistently rank highest in number of suicides.

8. Suicide rates are highest among individuals who are divorced or widowed and lowest among those who are married.

9. With youth and young adults, ages 15 to 24, suicide rates increased more than 200% from the 1950s to the late 1970s. Current rates are approximately still 200% higher than the 1950s.

10. Suicide ranks second only to accidents as a cause of death among youth and young adults, ages 15 to 24.

11. Suicide rates among whites are approximately twice that of non-whites.

12. Native Americans have the highest suicide rates overall. There are large differences, however, between tribes.

13. The majority of those who are suicidal display clues and warning signs.

14. It is estimated that at least 3.5 million Americans have had a loved one who committed suicide.

15. 50% of teenagers who attempt suicide have a depressed, suicidal mother.

16. 50% of adolescents who attempt suicide describe their family life as "on-going warfare."

17. 80% of patients who are medically treated for major depression attempt suicide within the first three months of improvement.

18. 95% of teenagers who attempt suicide survive.

19. Depressed students are often over looked because they are considered troublemakers.

---

8. Michigan Association of Suicidology. (1997).

# Suicide Assessment - SLAP Method

How **SPECIFIC** is the plan of attack? The more specific the details relate, the higher the degree of present risk.

How **LETHAL** is the proposed method? How quickly could the person die if the plan is implemented? The greater the level of lethality, the greater the risk.

How **AVAILABLE** is the proposed method? If the tool to be used is readily available, the level of suicide risk is greater.

What is the **PROXIMITY** of helping resources? Generally, the greater the distance the person is from helping resources, –if the plan were implemented, the greater the degree of risk.

*Warning:* Knowing the SLAP method does not necessarily make one an expert in assessing suicide risk!

**NOTE:** The SLAP Method was developed by Dr. Kenneth Morris.

## Suicide Causes

Suicide is *usually* not a result of one or a few isolated events in an individual's life, but the end of a series of extremely frustrating events. The main causes of suicide include:

- **Alcohol and/or other drug addiction.** *

- **Break up of family relationships.** *

- **Depression.**

- **Feelings of insecurity.**

- **Illness.**

- **Broken love affairs.**

- **Economic or business affairs that turn sour.**

- **Disfiguring injuries or disease.**

\* Indicates most common causes among teenagers.

# How to Recognize a Potentially Suicidal Individual

**Suicide–Prone Individuals:**

- Have poor self-esteem. They believe that no one loves them and that they cannot do anything right.

- Often are anti-social and isolate themselves. They often are introverted and become withdrawn.

- Frequently exhibit drastic changes in behavior.

- Will often times make open threats or lay clues for ending their life.

- May use alcohol or other drugs excessively.

- May show a change in a set of habits. Mostly these changes are related to their appearance.

- May give away prized possessions.

- Develop poor communication with family, friends and relatives.

- May have a history of prior suicide attempts.

- Are at higher risk if from families in which other suicides have occurred.

# Suicide: How We Can Help

- *Be a good listener.* Listen not only to what the person is saying, but also to what the person is not saying.

- *Evaluate the individual.* Does the person have a plan? Is the individual speaking in a rational way or just being emotional?

- *Do not suggest that the individual carry through with the plan.* What if the person heeded the advice? Reverse psychology is not a good approach with those contemplating suicide.

- *Accept every feeling and complaint the person expresses.* Do not argue with the individual and do not confirm suicide as an appropriate solution.

- *Do not be afraid to confront the person directly.* Ask if the individual is thinking about carrying through with the suicide.

- *Be aware of fast recoveries.* The person may just feel better because he or she has talked about it and may feel relieved that the decision not to commit suicide has been made.

- *Be supportive and affirmative.* Assure the individual that everything possible will be done to help.

- *Seek further consultation.* Recognize your personal limitations.

- *Help the person realize that suicide is irreversible.* A suicide cannot be undone. Suicide is a permanent solution to a temporary problem.

- *Remind the person that depressed feelings will pass.* Help the person realize that there is someone who cares about him or her. Help the person also realize that he or she does have something to offer. (A depressed individual usually will not want to listen to clichés, like "when the going gets tough, the tough get going."

- *Never leave the person alone in an acute crisis.* If the person has made a plan and appears serious, either go get help together, or leave the suicidal individual with someone else and go seek help.